T0149982

WINNING YOUR PARENTS' APPROVAL

divorce for

7 PRACTICES TO LEAVE YOUR MARRIAGE WITH THEIR BLESSING

CINDY A. GUNRAJ

CDC CERTIFIED DIVORCE COACH®

WINNING YOUR PARENTS' APPROVAL FOR DIVORCE
7 Practices to Leave Your Marriage with Their Blessing

CINDY A. GUNRAJ
CDC Certified Divorce Coach®

Difference Press, Washington, D.C., USA
© Cindy Gunraj, 2020

ISBN: 978-1-68309-258-2

Cover Design: Jennifer Stimson
Editing: Moriah Howell
Author's photo courtesy of: Kristal Passy LLC

DIFFERENCE
P R E S S

For my mom, for her big heart and beautiful smile that lights up this world. You always made our house feel like a home.

For my dad, for giving me your crazy work ethic, strong will, and belief in the divine spirit!

For David, the love of my life, who shows up with kindness, love, and respect, and is always my cool breeze on a hot day!

For Joy, you've taught me so much about bravery, love, and sweet connection.

Table of Contents

Chapter 1

Leave Your Marriage with Your Parents' Blessing

FEELING TRAPPED IN YOUR MARRIAGE

I know what it feels like when you don't seem to have control of your own life. It's like you're living this reality in which you please others, and get everything done, but your needs aren't getting met. You probably feel alone and like you're trapped in your marriage. You're taking care of your husband, the house, the chores, the kids, your family, organizing events, attending events, and all the while breaking down inside. You smile, look pretty, and make sure everything adds up on the outside, but inside, you're a total wreck. You feel anxious, worried, fearful, tired, and overwhelmed most of the time. Maybe like a chicken running with your head cut off! You just keep giving and giving, and your "well" is mostly empty. You don't feel like things are equal in this marriage. You feel like your husband doesn't see you, listen to you, and most of the time he's not even there! He's off in his own world where he gets an excuse to do what he wants when he wants, and he uses work to dodge anything.

He can be very critical of you if something isn't done to his liking. He finds faults in you and the way you do things. Perhaps it's your cooking, planning trips, your clothes, or not looking after the kids in just the right way. Sometimes he looks at you with cold eyes and a tight face like he's disgusted by you. He probably thinks you've lost your looks because he doesn't look at you with lust. He's closed that door for some time. He's always tired and exhausted; you haven't been intimate for a very long time. There's a disconnection with your body. You don't even know if you're worthy of being touched. You feel beaten down, and it seems like he rarely has anything positive to say to you anymore. You don't even greet each other when he walks in the door; there's this coldness and emotional emptiness. When you do talk, it's about the house, logistics, the kids, or maybe even in-laws. You can't stand him because he looks at and talks about other women. You feel so insecure and secretly think, "If only I were prettier." But you are also disgusted by him and resentful because he keeps breaking his promises. He promises to show up to the birthday, family event, or special time together but never does. Something important always comes up and his priority is his work. Your needs have been last for a very long time.

AFRAID OF YOUR PARENTS' REACTION

You're so done with this marriage and want to leave. But then it hits you: what will your parents think? They expect you to be a good and supportive wife. Your husband is working so hard for you and the family. He's been taking care of you for so long, and you owe him for working so hard. You shouldn't bother him with petty things like this. Your parents see this story in a very different way. They see it as you having freedom; he's a great provider, you're living a lavish lifestyle, and your children are getting the best things life has to offer.

But they don't know that you're having panic attacks, high anxiety, and lack of love in your marriage. They expect a lot from you, and you always deliver. You love your parents and want to make them so comfortable and happy. After all, they've done such a good job raising you, and they remind you how much they've done for you. They're so proud of your lifestyle. They brag about your kids and adore your husband. They've gone on trips with you, have stayed at your house for months at a time, and love hearing about how your husband's climbing the corporate ladder! So naturally, you're very scared to talk to your parents about leaving your marriage. They could get angry and be very hard on you, maybe even saying things like, "You're being so childish" or "You're disappointing us" or "You'll bring shame to this family with such a stupid thing." They could say, "Your needs don't matter – here, look how much is being done for you!" Then you'd have to deal with the consequences of this. They could hate you, and you would fall far down their list of approval.

JUGGLING ROLES AND READY FOR CHANGE

You've been juggling so much as a wife, mother, and daughter. It's breaking you. You feel so unhappy inside and anxious. A lot of the work has fallen on you to raise the kids, take care of the house, care for family, and make sure everything is looked after. You also feel like you're walking on eggshells in your own home. Your husband has shown how angry and cold he can get. He expects you to manage everything and dismissing you in an instant if anything goes wrong. You're tired, exhausted, drained, and feel so alone because you've realized you don't have a partnership. You have someone whose needs are getting taken care of and doesn't even stop to take a second look at you. There's this internal conflict between what everybody wants of you and what your heart says. You realize that you've sacrificed so much and it's hurting your soul to stay in your marriage. You keep expecting things to get better with your husband, and you keep getting let down. The pain is too much to endure anymore, and you're ready for a change.

LOYALTY TO YOUR PARENTS

You love your parents and they expect you to stay true to your commitments. They've invested so much in you to find the good husband, and even paid for the marriage. They've put so much emotional, physical, and financial labor into making this union happen. Both your husband's family and yours know each other so well, their roots have been intertwined. You've always tried your hardest to please your parents, and it hurts you when they're disappointed with you. So how do you leave this marriage without upsetting and disappointing your very traditional Indian parents?

GETTING PARENTS' BLESSING AND FREEDOM

Your real dream come true would be if your parents gave you their blessing and support to leave this marriage! If they were on your side, you would feel so supported. You would feel like you're not letting them down, and this would give you more confidence. They could guide you with the important decisions to leave the marriage. They could stand up for you and talk with his parents. They could make sure you were taken care of and pick you up when you are feeling low. Most of all, you wouldn't have to face disappointment from them and your community. You wouldn't bring shame and have immense guilt, because they would be in your corner! They could financially help you if things got really tough, and they would help you make decisions for the kids. You could spend more time taking care of yourself, and your mom would come to your rescue. She would probably pamper you because it's such a difficult thing to go through. You would feel lighter, brighter, and have more ease knowing that your parents could fight some of these battles for you. You could go through this process and get closer to your parents because they would also be there to be a sounding board and hold your hand.

This dream is possible! In this book, I'll show you how you can release this miserable marriage, and you can leave with pride and dignity. You can finally tell your husband good-bye! This will make you feel more empowered, and you'll have more time to spend on yourself. You'll be free from cooking his meals and looking after his needs when he doesn't even appreciate you. You can have more time to do things you'd like to do. Maybe you'll discover some new passions or try a new activity. You'll feel less anxious, have more mental space, and even feel better about yourself. You will feel like you wouldn't need to answer to him, listen to his criticisms, and feel unloved by him anymore. You will have peace of mind and your parents' love!

Chapter 2

Marriage Struggles and the Phoenix Rising

MY OWN MARRIAGE

It's so normal to feel scared about the future when you're considering leaving your marriage. There you are, staring at a possible new world where you know nothing, and it's filled with uncertainty. When you're thinking about divorce, it's not just one thing changing; it's connected to so many other things that make up your life. These are things like your in-laws, social circles, financial status, living environment, and your kids' lives and well-being. You could be feeling immense shame and guilt. Or maybe you feel more like a failure because it's not working out as you planned. You tried your hardest to communicate to your husband and feel seen in the relationship, but it's not working.

Looking back, I was unhappy, confused, and pretty darn anxious during my marriage. I found myself questioning my abilities, riddled with self-doubt, and had this growing worthlessness in the pit of my stomach. I would play these roles like good wife, good daughter-in-law, and good daughter to fill that void and make sure I was measuring up. But inside, I was still empty and was becoming a shell of a woman. All my qualities were stripping away as I was trying my best to force myself into these roles and make others happy. Does this sound like you?

You have to really examine your marriage in its entirety. Do you all bring out the best in each other? Do you feel like you work through conflicts, or are you all avoiding real issues? Do you feel your worst most of time when you're together? For the majority of the marriage, I was definitely on the lower end of the spectrum of feeling peace and happiness. My husband continued to amplify my insecurity because I later realized that he was not a normal communicator. He talked in circles, went back on promises, was absent for most of our marriage, and if anything went wrong, was very comfortable with blaming me. Maybe you've experienced some of this with your husband. Maybe it's driving you crazy because you feel like you're stuck, and you can't seem to do anything right. For example, when we separated, I asked him what could I do to fix this. He said, "You should know I don't want kids." I said, "How would I know that if you don't tell me?" He told me I should read his mind.

Through therapy, I was beginning to see his expectations were really ridiculous. He had a very difficult time grasping my needs or showing empathy and compassion. Everything always seemed to be my fault. If something went wrong with our house, he would say, "Well, you're the one who wanted the house." Things seemed to always be turned around on me. I felt fearful to go to him for anything and felt like I was living in fight-or-flight mode for so long.

Of course, my whole marriage wasn't this abyss of terribleness. There was connection, laughter, exploration, and love. I remember learning so much from my mother-in-law and my sister-in-law. They were fantastic cooks, planners, and hosts and embraced me by sharing their traditions. I got a chance to dive into my Indian roots by learning more about the religion, food, music, and got to witness their beautiful family bonds. That experience enriched me in a way that I'm so grateful for. I can now say that being on the other side of my divorce!

WANTING MY HUSBAND'S APPROVAL, RESPECT, AND LOVE

My marriage started feeling like a burden. My husband worked, traveled a lot, and seem uninterested in our relationship. It was like living with a roommate that you hardly saw. For years, I pushed it down and ignored it, hoping things would get better in my marriage. My husband wouldn't listen to me when I voiced my concerns.

Years of feeling unseen physically, mentally, and emotionally broke me down. My face flared up with acne, my hair fell out, and I was feeling so worthless. Have you experienced this stress coming out physically? It can be weight gain, lack of sleep, nausea, racing heart, or a tense body. Take stock of what's happening with you physically because your inner world is connecting to your outer world.

I felt like I was stuck in a house living with someone engrossed in work, accolades, striving, and wanting to impress his parents. I was at the very bottom of his list, but I didn't really know it at the time. I thought I wasn't living up to his expectations of me. I wished he would be happy with me; I wished he would look at me in a special way. To make matters worse, my husband talked about how special other women were. Work colleagues, his mother, his sister... I was being put in a position where I had to compete to prove my worthiness to be with him. I tried; I dressed well, kept the house beautiful, shopped for all the wonderful things he liked, took his parents around, and I really enjoyed building the bonds with them. I wanted him to see that I could fit it to his world.

I was hoping I would someday meet my husband's expectations. I so desperately wanted his approval, his respect. After all, he talked highly about his job, work accomplishments, and how great he was. I, too, wanted to measure up. But it was never going to happen. Why?

We were both mirroring lack within us. My desire for him to fill a void within me and him trying to fill a void within himself.

UNABLE TO OWN MY OWN VOICE

One of my internal struggles was not being able to own my own voice. Growing up, I saw my mom and aunts yelling and arguing from the top of their lungs. Then they would get it out of their system, leave it alone, and flare up again. It was watching a vicious cycle of the same fight that never gets solved! The women I grew up around didn't know how to use their voices in order to make real change happen. Also, their husbands certainly didn't encourage it. My husband and I fell into a cycle where I flared up, he ignored me, and I went back to pretending everything was fine. That's also why I stayed in the relationship for so long. I didn't know this was a dysfunctional way of communicating; it was our normal. A big struggle of mine was changing the way I communicate, and this broke the cycle.

How do the women in your family respond to challenges with their partner? Are they able to stand up for themselves in a productive way? Do they seem to dance around conflict and seethe in silence? Do they give their partner the silent treatment and avoid talking about the issue? Notice how your mom and the women around you solve disagreements with their partners. This will help you see if this influences your own style of communication with your partner.

DYING ON THE INSIDE

Another internal struggle was maintaining the outside and dying on the inside. I was feeling trapped and lonely living a lie painted on the outside. I'd checked off all the boxes: nice house, good provider, nice things, good family, but it wasn't sustaining my spirit. Are you living a life where it looks good on the outside, but it feels so empty inside the walls of your home? I was going along with things to make my husband happy and maybe you find yourself doing the same thing. You think, "Well, I couldn't get him to listen to my needs, and I pretend that is okay by overcompensating on the outside."

I was not in control of my life and my own decision-making. I was seen as a piece fitting a bigger system that was working, and I need to do my duties in order for this huge system to work! Do you feel like you're supporting this huge system, and you're just a worker bee taking orders? Maybe you feel like your voice, opinions, and wants are falling on deaf ears. Perhaps you've had a bunch of arguments with your husband about wanting to spend more time together. But he continues to spend his free time on sports, events, evening dinners, traveling, and whatever else he deems important. I experienced this, and after a while, felt so discarded and insignificant.

GOING TO CALIFORNIA

Life has your back, even when it doesn't seem like it. My husband had the bright idea for me to move to California for me to try my hand at acting. He said I needed to go because I supported him for years and I should do this for myself. Now, I'd gone to acting school and done a few plays and short movies, but surely wasn't pursuing it fulltime. I always made myself available for our marriage, and my allegiance was in supporting his rise and my duties as a wife. If you had a spouse who was both in school and work for most of your relationship, then you'll understand that a lot of the household duties would naturally fall on you. We had just bought a house and the next logical step was starting a family. Going to California didn't make sense to me, and I was so afraid to leave him. But he was determined for me to go. I went because I thought this would be good for us.

When I was away, he became more distant and was thinking about leaving the marriage. In fact, I was the one making an effort to talk with him and booked his tickets to see me; it seemed like something was off. I had alarm bells ringing in my mind. I returned to New York because my intuition was also telling me it was time to return home.

Here is a key lesson – always listen to your intuition. Intuition can be a gut feeling when something is off; it's like a whisper or a signal trying to tell you something.

These whispers start off as a small nudge, a faint sound, and when you don't listen, they manifest into a knock over the head! Your intuition is always guiding you to better things for yourself. It's your future self guiding you to take this step, and it also gives you warning signals in the process.

I had many of these in my marriage, but chose to ignore them. My husband was thinking about leaving the marriage for some time, and he needed a way out. I messed up his plans with my return. It wasn't too long before my return when he told me that he wanted to separate. He said he's been burdened, we'd taken on too many expenses too quickly, and he wanted to unpack everything and start over. At least, that was what he told me at the time.

We separated and I went into therapy where I learned so much about myself. I learned that I was not in a healthy marriage and I needed to leave. I learned that I wasn't such a burden, uncaring, un-thoughtful person. I learned that I was trying to do my best to please and make my husband happy. But it was never going to be enough and I was losing my soul in the process. That was my light bulb moment. I needed to do something differently to save my soul. I chose to pull my energy away from trying to make this marriage work to trying to learn about my past decisions and myself. How the heck did I get here? Do you ever think, "Why is this happening to me?" Well, this was my defining moment to be someone else and choose myself for once.

My husband wasn't prepared for the person I was becoming. He tried to find ways to make amends, communicate, and make me feel bad about our separation. Maybe you have a husband who blames you, says he's feeling so depressed and can't handle too much, and expects you to make it all better. He says if you do this thing or that thing it will be all better. But then his happiness depends on you, and if you fail him, you're automatically a bad person in his eyes. Is your husband cold towards you, quickly unforgiving, and puts his own needs in front of yours? Do you find yourself feeling out of balance? I know I did, and it was so humbling to free myself from that situation.

MY PARENTS' REACTION

My parents were unsupportive about the separation. I told my mom we were having issues in our marriage. She said, "Well, how often are you all having sex? Is he seeing someone else? How long has this been going on?" Her questions felt like darts to my heart, like I was on trial and had to walk on eggshells as I answered. Looking back, I can see I had poor boundaries with my parents. It's like they could ask me anything, infiltrating my life with one glance. How is your communication with your parents? I want you to take stock of this as we move through the chapters. Your current communication with them will determine how you should approach them with this topic. The funny thing was my communication with my parents – critical, blaming, judgmental, worried, and panicked – were the same things I experienced with my husband.

My parents could not understand why we were separating; they said I needed to fix my marriage. They said I made a commitment, and I needed to stick it out like they did. But how could I fix something that I never had control of in the first place? You're probably thinking; if you had control over your husband, you wouldn't be reading this book! I saw that my parents weren't listening to me. My dad cried and started reciting the Bible loudly and in sheer panic. He made it seem like this was my fault. He said he was disappointed in me and that was so difficult for me. I felt like I was disappointing everyone, and this was a defining moment for me. I could either crumble under pressure from my parents, but I chose to go to therapy, work on myself, and see how I could fix this. What I realized was that I was the one always giving in relationships and falling for the traps of people's wants.

PHOENIX RISING

We were changing in two different directions, and my heart wanted me to honor that. It was scary, but for me it was also the best decision of my life! I got a chance to spend time alone and develop my intuition. I meditated a lot, spent time in nature, and was asking for the Divine spirit to guide me through my divorce with grace and love. California was a wonderful precursor to this because I got time to build confidence in myself and create headspace. Those six months were actually the best thing that could have happened, because they set the foundation of inner strength and trust.

I remember going to Agape church in Culver City because my intuition was telling me something was wrong in my relationship. I couldn't understand why my husband became so distant when he urged me to do this. Isn't this want he wanted? I remember feeling so uplifted in Agape, and it was what my heart needed. I felt my grandmother and my ancestors in that space. They were all telling me that I was going to be fine, and I started crying. Tears flowing among these strangers who all seemed familiar to me in some way. This experience was preparing me for the difficult road ahead. This is what I mean about life having your back. What seems like a setback is really setting you up for the road ahead.

You just don't know how life will turn around to support you. You have to trust the process and trust what your heart wants. My divorce was tough, but I was more prepared for it. My husband hired a tough litigator to intimidate me, and in his eyes I deserved nothing. I learned very quickly that I was dealing with a liar, bully, and someone who had been whispering lies in my ears all these years. My therapist helped me see what I was really in, and this was pivotal in helping me protect myself.

Maybe you can relate, and it's waking you up to some dark crevices in your own life. This is a time where you should start to think about your needs, protecting yourself, and seeing what really is important to you.

I learned not to put myself in positions to take other peoples' worries on. It was like I was learning how to protect my wellness so that I could operate at my best for my own health. My mom used to say we can't do that because it's a selfish thing to do, but I learned that was a lie. If we are trying desperately to meet other peoples' needs by betraying ourselves and sacrificing our own needs, then who is really benefiting here? Who is really selfish here? Do you find yourself getting bad advice from your inner circle? I would start to question, "Is this advice true for me?" Also, examine where it's coming from, because it's usually based out of fear and limited to that person's experience. Loved ones can be wonderful in a divorce, or they can scare you half to death!

To clear all the external noise, I would spend time alone. Here I could self-reflect, hearing my thoughts, the crazy talking in my brain, and really started diving deep to change that stuff, and those are some key reasons why I was able to successfully leave my marriage. I want you to take stock of what's going on in your head. What kind of thoughts are you having? Are they making you feeling good? Are you anxious, worried, and beating yourself up? Start to get curious, because it will help you through this process.

I was building my confidence in my inner strength and my resilience. I really took ownership of taking care of me and putting myself first. Another key that I learned was showing up for me first before I solved any problem. I was going to eat well, take rest, reflect, and I was going to talk to a trusted person who had my best interests at heart. Then I was going to make my decision from that place. I wasn't going to be bullied, forced, manipulated, or threatened.

LET GO OF HEAD TRASH

I learned about taking care of myself by talking nicely to myself. Being easy on myself was going to make me feel much better than if I chose the other route. Then, I had extra to give because I'd taken care of me. That was one of the hardest lessons in leaving my marriage, but it was the key to setting me free and stepping into my new role. I learned to "let go of head trash." It's those internal gremlins that tell me I'm not good enough, I shouldn't do this, I don't deserve this, and so forth. I learned to let go of it by building more confidence in myself. I learned to take a step toward standing up for my heart. This lovely heart that was guiding me towards my highest self the whole time. I was so afraid to listen because it would mean some big things would need to change.

My parents saw that I was changing. I would tell them honestly and openly what my heart was feeling. I would say, "I'm not feeling up to talking about this. I'm not feeling up to doing this. I need to recharge my battery, so I need to step away. Please don't fight in my house." I was exercising my boundaries and voicing my opinions. At first, this was startling to them, because they'd never heard it before. But when they saw it was coming from a real, grounded place, they stopped and listened. It was alarming for me at first, but I saw that all the work I was doing – yoga, therapy, writing about my feelings, going in nature and spending time alone, going through the divorce proceedings – all of this was building character and giving me depth. I was starting to really believe in myself, and my parents took note of that. I was no longer someone who was confused, needed to be looked after, and fixed in their eyes. It's like the field was being leveled, and respect was being earned. But it didn't come from them, it came from inside me and then showed in the outside world. I needed to learn how to have respect for myself first so I could model that to others.

HOW I CAN HELP YOU

I'm the perfect person to help women who are ready to leave their marriage, but are scared to death. I'm the perfect person because I've done it in a big way. I've had to show up and face cultural issues, the wrath of my parents, and the lost of my in-laws. I've had to leave a world of total physical comforts – nice house, comfy bank account, respected Indian family, successful husband – and had to rebuild from the ground up. I had the three major life changes happen all at once: change of career, change of living, and change of relationship status. These were layered with challenging my own family self-doubts and being looked down upon by my culture as the "women who got left."

My fighting spirit dug deep to change this story and recreate a new chapter. A chapter filled with authentic love, a life where I live my life on my own terms, I love myself and all my flaws, I'm free from other's opinions of me, and where I've taken the time to uncover my own passion and gifts. Where I've learn to spend time alone and love my own company. I love being with my thoughts. I've even traveled to different countries on my own. That was one of the biggest taboos in my culture, that it's not safe for women to travel alone and be alone.

I had to get rid of all that head trash, and the way I did it was by stepping out of my comfort zone! Because of my choice to leave my marriage, I've discovered so much richness about me. I have pride in myself and walk with a strong stride. People know when I'm in the room, not because I'm cocky, but because my presence is so engulfing and attractive. I've been told I light up a room because I'm so easy to talk to, that I'm such a good motivator, and I see things that other people don't. All of this is because I took a chance to leap and believe in my own worthiness.

What's beautiful is my mom looks up to me now. She's thrilled that I became so strong, independent, and attracted a *real* partnership. She looks at me with a sparkle in her eye and my heart tells me that she loves what I've accomplished. Why? Because in her time, it was nearly impossible, and I did what she could only dream of doing back then. I'm living my life on my own terms and doing work that inspires her. It's amazing how things come full circle. My work is closing a gap for the women in my culture.

Chapter 3

The Road Map to Leaving Your Marriage

I've been through an amazing journey to self-acceptance to realizing things about my external environment. I really had to walk the walk to get me here in order to write this book for you. It wasn't an easy feat by any stretch of the imagination, and you're getting a taste of it because you're in the beginning stages. I do want to let you know that it is very possible for yourself. It's so possible to have the life you want, to create happiness, to have a bounce in your step! To learn to love yourself and feel a sense of appreciation for your own presence. I'm not saying this happens overnight; there is a specific series of practices I uncovered to help me leave my marriage. I'm going to share them with you through this framework so you can be ready to leave your marriage.

CLEARING CULTURAL CONFUSION AND FACING YOUR FUTURE

The first thing is that you really want to clear the confusion. When we don't clear the confusion everything gets blended together, and you feel hopeless, unsure of your right next step. Specifically we'll look at what cultural blocks are keeping you stuck and from moving forward. I call it cultural confusion and it's like living in a gray cloud; it prevents you from seeing the right decisions for you. You may feel that you're bound to duty, loyalty, tradition, and little nuances. You body and heart may feel at war with each other where an inner tension arises. Maybe you heard growing up that woman don't go out by themselves or they're supposed to do all the domestic housework and not ask for help. Looking at cultural blocks will help you see where you feel limited, unequal to others, and suppress your voice. Then, you'll need to find out what's important about having your parents blessing in order to leave the marriage. We're going to dive into that, set up a foundation to do that, and you're going to get clarity quickly. You'll uncover nuggets that'll help direct you and make you feel more confident, so you know where to go. This will help you see the future staring at you and you'll get a very clear picture so you know how to navigate.

YOUR PARENTS' PAST IS BURIED TREASURE!

Next, we will really dig deep and uncover the parental relationship and your parental dynamics. This means we will be looking closely at your relationship with your parents so you know how to navigate this change with them. For example, are they easy to talk to with really important things? Are they critical of you? Do you feel like you're walking on eggshells with them? Do you have to watch what you say to avoid judgment? Avoid conflict with them? Maybe you're splitting your hairs trying to do your best to make sure they are happy. This stuff is so important because it leads to knowing how you operate with your parents and how you operate with yourself.

CONSCIOUS UNCOUPLING

Another practice to ending a marriage is finding your real intentions or real purpose for leaving. This helps to clear the noise, to get to your underlying bedrock intention or your "why." When you connect to your "why," it's like a North star that guides you in dark times. It makes you see things very clearly, and you live from a place where you're connected to your God. It's vital to do the work to uncover your real intentions.

KNOW WHAT DECISION IS RIGHT AND NOT RIGHT FOR YOU

Then we're going to look at how do you know which decision is right for you and which one is not. It's important to hone this skill so you stay true to yourself. You can learn to balance your needs with the needs of others. This means really seeing what decisions you're making and what actions you're taking that are preventing you from moving towards your bigger purpose of leaving this marriage. When you know the right decision, you move with more intention, you make intentional choices, and you feel like you can do this because you're getting to know yourself. You're also not hiding from yourself anymore, and you trust yourself and trust your judgment, and you're not going to betray yourself.

ENVISIONING LEAVING THE MARRIAGE

Next, we will look at envisioning leaving the marriage and knowing where you're going. This is so important because it sets up the possibility of seeing something. When you're in a tunnel of darkness, you'll hold on to that vision you've created for yourself. You'll visualize what benefits you're receiving when you left the marriage. What experiences are you having? It's really about getting in touch with that space to help you move forward. It's so important to dive into that field of awareness. Think of it as calling your future-self forward. You see the possibilities; she's making her own decisions and living life on her own terms. Then you have a sparkle in your eyes because you felt what the future feels like! It does something to your cells and lights up your heart.

It expands your inner strength and beautiful qualities because you've already seen it, touched it, tasted it, and smelled it! This space is oh so sweet, and it's just waiting for you to claim it.

PREPARING TO LEAVE – TRANSITION MOJO, FIVE BIGGEST MISTAKES, AND HOLIDAY BLUES

Next, we'll dive into transition mojo – it's the discipline required to make a change. When you're going through a transition, you need to have focus, investment, commitment, and you need to be 100 percent in for it to be successful. Afterward, we'll uncover the five biggest mistakes women make when they're thinking about leaving their marriage. These pitfalls are detrimental to them because they cripple them. I'm going to share the details and how to maneuver so you don't fall into those traps. These five things were pivotal for me in becoming a leader, trusting myself, and learning why it's important to put myself first in this process. This rapidly increased my health, well-being, gave me peace within, and allowed me to face challenges with confidence. I'm so thrilled to share these with you! We'll wrap up with looking at how holidays and events can bring you down. You'll feel obligated to attend holidays, birthdays, and religious events that involve your spouse and his family. We'll look at how to navigate this so you stay on your path.

WHO'S ON YOUR TEAM? CREATE THE RIGHT SUPPORT CIRCLES.

Then we will uncover the importance of having the right support circle when you're thinking about leaving your marriage. You'll need the right support to take this leap. Connecting with supportive role models and social circles is key because it will fill you and sustain you in your decisions. You'll also meet like-minded people and feel more like leaving your marriage is a possibility. Finding the right support circles could look like stepping out of your culture to experience other cultures' thinking. Having the right people in your corner is critical to leaving your marriage because these folks are going to be your cheerleaders. They are going to inspire you and give you hope.

TAKE THE LEAP AND DIVINE COMMUNICATION

The last step is to take the leap and this is the decision to leave the marriage. This is sharing your feelings and decisions with others, releasing attachments to any outcomes. Here you would be equipped with all the tools to take the plunge to have a difficult conversation and to really face your parents with more confidence and clarity. Things will shake you, but at the same time, there's the excitement of the possibility of moving towards your dreams. You would have learned about yourself, been doing work to take the leap, and you'll have built in systems to help you manage this decision. You also would've already been taking small steps to feel more like yourself and feel like you have tools to navigate leaving your marriage.

The steps I've set forth are going to give you the confidence and resilience to face challenges and know that you are going to be ok no matter what happens! Here you would be also creating the space to deepen the bonds with your parents. You'll show them that you're ready to leave, they don't have to worry about you, and that you care for them deeply. You want them to join you in this journey.

Chapter 4

Clearing Cultural Confusion and Facing Your Future

THE ROLES YOU PLAY IN YOUR CULTURE

How are you influenced by your culture, roles, and your parents' relationship? Think about the traditions you carry out, your rituals, the roles you see between genders and the various roles one can play being a wife, mother, and daughter-in-law. These things were not so black and white for me at first. I didn't understand that things were suddenly shaping my behavior and me. For example, I didn't really understand the separate roles women and men played in my culture until later on in my life. I knew boys hung out with boys. They were allowed to go out, explore, stay out late, fight, and, when they became teenagers, some drank heavily. I remember a few of my uncles drinking until they lost consciousness! Did you witness boys having more freedom with their time and leeway to try things? If so, I want you think about how that has shaped you now.

Also, did your culture have lots of religious functions, festivities, with loads of people? Mine did, and sometimes there was easily over a 100 people! There was loud music, lots of dancing, drinks, food, and it was really a great time. Have you been around this kind of atmosphere? It can be intoxicating and fun! But it was also an opportunity for some to drink their troubles away. Things like fights, family squabbles, and gossiping were totally normal. Your privacy becomes a rare thing, because all of sudden family members had loose lips and shared your personal stories. Did you experience this kind of embarrassment? Telling each other's stories was a sort of bonding, but it also was common to violate someone's privacy. Maybe you've felt that and it's caused you to think twice before disclosing your personal feelings to loved ones.

YOUR CULTURE'S QUIRKS

Moreover, my culture had loads of quirks, and perhaps you'll relate to some of these. For example, if you didn't show up to all the family events you received many tongue-lashings. What does that mean? You were looked at as anti-social, or relatives would say, "You miss out and really should have been there!" There was a clannish mentality where you *had* to go along with crowd. Family members would guilt trip you into feeling bad for not showing up. They said, "Why weren't you there? Everyone was asking for you. What happened? Is everything okay?" It was like one big brain operating when I look back on it.

My culture also loves bright colors, flashing things, looking good, talking about what you own, and always trying your best to one up each other. It was common for our parents to say things like, "Why can't you be like so-and-so's son or daughter? How could you let your cousin beat you in their test scores?" Can you see how this environment influenced my low self-esteem? Perhaps this is resonating and setting off a few light bulbs for you. This was a breeding ground for comparison, pinning siblings against one another, and a lot of guilt and shame emerged in this environment. I always felt like I was lacking in some way. If it wasn't school, it was my looks. There was always something to aspire to in order to measure up. But that thing never lasted! Maybe you feel this way, too. This can be so stifling to your personal growth! I have to say, though, that there was beauty in this craziness. At the end of the day, we did have each other's backs and enjoyed celebrating with each other. We loved our traditions, food, rituals, music, and there was a kind of kinship in all this twisted up behavior.

THE FEMALE RAT RACE

Growing up, the girls danced a different tune than the boys. Were you treated differently because of your gender? I know I was! We were groomed to learn domestic skills! For example, they were quickly directed to help out in the kitchen, set the dining table, decorate, clean and be pulled to do a lot of one-off tasks. Another thing, girls often served as their mom's emotional support system. What does that mean? Moms would confide hurts to them sometimes without boundaries. I remember being my mom's therapist where she confided to me the very tough times with my dad. How he would yell at her, call her stupid, and make her feel small. I also witness this on a daily basis, so it was pretty normal for them to bump heads. Of course, I didn't know how this was affecting me then. Can you think back to how your parents behaved around you? How did that affect you and how does it play out in your relationship?

THE RESCUER

I listened to my mom, tried to make her feel better, and spent time trying to build her up when she wasn't feeling good. Other times, she would be angry, yelling, and it was like walking on eggshells trying to get back on her good side. She would say things like, "No one takes me out, no one cares about me, no one appreciates what I do." She would get so angry if I didn't spend "enough time with her." It was sort of a guilt trip: "Oh, you're too busy for your mom. Why aren't you coming earlier or staying longer? Why didn't you call me? I tried calling you a couple of times." I would have just talked to her yesterday!

This was really hard to hear because no matter how hard I tried to make her feel better, another compliant would appear. She also was notorious for saying things like, "Why can't you be more like your sister?" or "Your brother took us here." We siblings had our doses of being compared to each other and falling short! Did this happen to you? Does it still happen to you? Later in life, I realized that I was put in place very early on to play the role of rescuer. Why? Because my mom felt helpless, hopeless, and like a victim most of the time. Can you relate to this? Are you perhaps playing this role with your parents?

LAUGHING OFF ABUSE

It was quite common for the women in my culture to be emotionally and physically abused. I remember my very first childhood memory was looking up at my mom and she had a black eye. One of my aunts joked, saying, "Your mom got another black-eye-pea." The women joked about it as a way of making light or minimizing the pain. It's amazing what sticks in your memory as a child. Do you have similar experiences in your childhood? Did you witness things that you couldn't make sense of at the time but knew that there was heaviness around you? I know this may seem so difficult to do, and perhaps you don't even want to go there. Maybe you blocked that stuff out or found a way to brush it off and move on. But that is where the nuggets of gold are, and it's the stuff that will help set you free. I've found that stuff sticks with you if it's not looked at. It influenced me in my relationship choices and how I saw myself as a woman.

ARRANGED MARRIAGE

The sad thing for the women in my culture was they were encouraged to marry early, discouraged from furthering their education, and choosing to live a single life was totally unheard of. My mom said living alone as a woman was seen unsafe because they wouldn't be able to protect themselves. In her time, she said women were easily raped if they were alone, shootings were more prevalent, and they needed male protection. This sounded so savage to me and made me thankful for the space I grew up in. Did your parents live thorough some crazy stuff? I know mine did.

Speaking of shootings, my cousin told me the story of how my mother brought my dad to her house for the first time. After that, my grandfather pulled a gun on him and told him he needed to marry his daughter! If a female was seen with males, she was a given name like "loose," "slut," or "easy," and then she would not be good marriage material. One goal of traditional Indian parents was to find good partners for their children. So they often asked around, observed, and sized up the material status of men. Why? Because marriage was more of an economical contract than a love one. Is this striking a chord with you? All of these helped me understand why my parents think the way they do and why they make certain choices with raising us.

Hence, arranged marriage was acceptable in my culture. Some of my aunts got married in their early teens as young as thirteen. They needed to find a provider, settle down, and support their family. Some even had in-laws to take care of and a heap of domestic responsibilities right away. It took time and energy to shop, cook, look after kids, run the house, all while making sure your husband's needs were taken care of as well. There was no time for a self-discovery journey here; these women had work to do! Did you experience this with the women in your culture? Maybe you saw them feeling like they had their life chosen for them. Maybe you even feel like that.

A cultural taboo was allowing women to manage the finances and make major financial decisions. They were told to not bother with it and sometimes excluded from the process entirely. Does this strike a chord with you? Some women were even given an allowance and looked at it as having "security" because they were married. So this set up a situation where women didn't really have rights and had to really depend on their husbands for their own livelihood. Can you relate to this? I know it was pretty easy for me to fall into that comfort zone of supporting my husband and his rise in his career. I remember his parents acknowledging how much I'd contributed to the marriage. They said, "We don't know what our son would have done without you." He'd been in school and work for most of our marriage! The funny thing is, I really didn't think much of his parents' comment because putting my needs aside to support him was my comfort zone. My own mother valued my dad's contributions way more than her own. Maybe this is you right now? I saw it as I was contributing in a small way, and he was doing all the heavy lifting. Maybe you've propelled your partner forward in his career by doing the heavy lifting at home.

YOU'RE SO SELFISH

Another cultural taboo was women aren't supposed to treat themselves, be nice to themselves, and make time for themselves. Can you feel me on this one? That was seen as indulging and being selfish. I remember my aunts and mom would be completely available for the family's needs. Even if they were tired, not feeling well, and just plain exhausted, they all made sure to have a hot meal on the table. If a woman did something nice for herself, the other women would give a warning, or poke fun saying things like, "Oh, you got away. Must be nice... you're so lucky. Don't leave your husband home alone too long!" Have you witnessed women doing so little for themselves? Maybe you're in that boat, feeling too selfish to do a little self-care. When you fill your cup up, you were seen as being selfish, weak, bragging, or foolish. Back then, there was no such thing as women going away for girls' get-aways, yoga retreats, or even having a quiet space to call their own! Their minds were trained to be at the beckon call of the family. Some men also hated when their wives spent money on themselves, and that reinforced their lack of self-worth and feeling incompetent with money. How have you seen this cycle play out in your own culture? How has it caused setbacks in your own life?

COMEDY HOUR ABOUT YOUR CHILDREN

A cultural quirk I experienced was how parents talked about their children's shortcomings. They bragged about their kids, but they also tried to one up each other by sharing negatives. Did you experience this with the elders in your family? I remember sitting around my aunts and they gossiped about how this child was lazy, had a bad temper, liked to complain, and was difficult to live with. Did you feel this too in your culture? It seems to make them feel like they all had common struggles. I know they looked for each other to have comfort the only problem was the news then spread like wildfire among the extended family. This is important to note because it plays into the fear of you wanting their approval and why you've kept stuff from them. Make sense? Only sharing the good stuff would get us the respect, admiration and bragging rights. I know this is one of the reasons I taught myself not to confide in my parents. There was no trust, it would be leaked to extended families. But this felt so lonely, especially when I was facing big life decisions like divorce! Do you feel this invasion of your privacy with your own family?

YOUR PARENTS' SUPPORT

Explore what's important to you about having your parents' blessing in order to leave your marriage. To get clear on this, answer a series of questions below:

- What are my biggest desires for having their support?
- What will I gain, and in what way will this move me forward?
- What will they give me that I can't already give myself?
- Is there a cost to having my parents support and blessing?
- What does that look like?
- Will I be indebted to them in some way?
- What happens if I don't receive their support?

- How will waiting for their support affect my future?
- What does this mean long term for me?
- What happens when I need to make future decisions and they aren't around?
- How will navigating this decision affect my future decisions?
- Who am I without my parents?
- Who am I outside of the role of wife and mother?
- Am I ready to move forward without their support?
- How could that terrain look?
- How could I best prepare myself?

Answering these questions will help you formulate your next step. You also see what thoughts are coming up and get a chance to examine them. These questions will help you dive into self-reflection and help you see what's really important to you. You'll also see what fears are holding you back, and that's half the battle. For me, I felt a rushing river of fears. Fears like I don't want to disappoint them and I don't want to do this alone. They know what's best for me and my identity was wrapped up in what they thought about me. Another fear of mine was being out in the cold with nothing after my divorce. If that happen where would I go? At least I would have my parents to count on to get me through this. They could help me make important decisions along the way. They could be a voice for me and make sure I wasn't taken advantage of. They could stand up for my rights and I would feel safe. I'd feel guilty bring shame to them if I did this on my own. Are you having similar worries and fears?

I looked at the importance of all this and why it needed to happen. I named the fears one by one, and I realized that this was not my reality. Write down your fears and see how you can take one step to move towards them. I know that sounds scary, but it's also how you build resilience and face the elephant in the room! This is a good time to take stock of how your parents react when you share important things with them. When I shared things with them in the past, they would freak out and be critical of me. As I mentioned earlier, my dad lost it when I told him we were separating. There was no way I was going to be able to count on them to guide me through this. When I came to this realization, it rocked me. I felt like this was an added battle, and that I couldn't take them along for this ride because it would be more stress on me. Maybe you're starting to see we have similar stories here. I had to be careful what to share because they were going through their own divorce or death of this marriage in their own way. I could only see this when I worked through my own feelings about my transition. This is why it's important to dive into self-reflection, because it puts you in a place to see bigger connections.

HOW IS THIS LIMBO PERIOD AFFECTING YOU?

You might be waiting in the wings to talk to your parents about this. Maybe you gently prodded them to hear their thoughts on this. Maybe you've told them and they gave you a flat out no! Whatever the case, you're waiting in some shape or form for your parents to come on board with you. Your parents may or may not agree with you, so the bigger question is to see how this is affecting you. Specifically, let's look at what it's been costing you to stay in this marriage.

Staying in my marriage was costing me my voice, my freedom to be me and to feel good about myself, to feel love, appreciation, and to feel admired. It was giving me huge anxiety and causing me to doubt myself at every turn. I started bursting into tears when my husband would complain about something going wrong with our rental property. I was the manager, so of course whenever we had issues with the tenant, it was my fault. I was so worn down and beaten down emotionally that it felt like I was walking on eggshells. Is this you? Do you feel like the quality of your life has taken a huge plummet? Do you feel like you're living in fear and self-doubt in this marriage? Does the majority of the time with your spouse feel like you're getting a root canal?

ANJALI LIFE

Now let me tell you a story of Anjali. On the outside, Anjali seemed like she had everything: a beautiful house, success, loving husband, and loads of money. She had three smart and beautiful children. Her family traveled internationally, working their way through Europe on the kids' vacations. Anjali's kids went to the best schools and were immersed in an array of afterschool activities. She had a nanny who cleaned, helped her cook, and did errands for her. She met other mothers at their social clubs, and they are part of a foundation that supports women empowerment.

Now, let's look closer at Anjali's life behind closed doors. She hardly spent time with her husband because he was gone for work most of the time. When he was at home, the house was filled with tension. He went through a bottle of Jonnie Walker Blue weekly to deal with the stress of work. He dismissed her with his looks, called her incompetent, and constantly told her she was doing a poor job as a wife and mother. She tried to calm him down, change the subject, and left the room if his insults got too bad. If he drank, he ended up picking a fight. He got in her face and stood over her, intimidating her. He felt comfortable grabbing her and shaking her, and his eyes cut through her bones. She saw he was totally checked out with rage, and one false move assured her that her life was on the line. She froze and listened to his demanding voice. Her primary way of being was feeling anxious, unworthy, and hopeless around him. But she didn't know it because she'd been operating like this for decades. She was too ashamed to tell people what was going on because she thought it's all her fault. Because he told her she wanted this lifestyle, and his pain was her fault. It's her duty to make him feel better, to lift him up because he was so stressed. There was nothing left for her because she used it on him. But she can't see that. Why? Because it was all about him. He talked about work, his worries, his needs, and his accomplishments. The communication was always centered around him. If they were intimate, it was when he wanted it. He was used to calling the shots in every arena of their life, and that was all she knew. She felt trapped.

What is it costing you to stay in your marriage? What's your primary way of being? Have you been doing it a certain way for so long that you've forgotten what happiness looks like for you?

YOU'RE MORTAL

What are your future costs for staying in this marriage? You need to look at the big picture and see how much longer can you go on like this. What will it do to your health, your wellbeing, your soul, and what kind of person will you show up as? You're not going to be around forever. Women often make the mistake of waiting it out, but time is ticking away. Your life is ticking away. Looking at the future with my husband scared me more than looking at the future without him. But it wasn't until I uncovered that he spent time with an ex-girlfriend in the midst of our separation did that wake me up. I remember it clearly, my intuition coming in to say, "Cindy, how much more of this are you going to take?" I was seeing our marriage wasn't filled with love. It was filled with avoidance, loneliness, no emotional connection, neediness, no trust, and unfaithfulness on both our parts, lack of intimacy, lying, and a deep longing for something or someone else. I saw that this relationship was not for me anymore. This incident was a sting that woke me up, and it made me see that I don't really like who I am when I'm with this man. How did I know that? Because I'd touched into that space of that future woman. The woman who was calling me to a higher way of being filled with possibility.

TAPPING INTO YOUR SWEET SPOT

I remember feeling beautiful when I got back from LA, but after being in the house again, everything came rushing back. The stare from my husband making me feel subpar, and his disgusted looks and furrowed brow. It was like slaps in the face to any self-esteem I gathered during that time away. I was back to feeling reprimanded and spoken to like a little child when the slightest thing went wrong. Understanding what it was costing me to stay in that marriage was huge. Why? It gave me permission to walk away. Being away from him allowed me to see parts of myself that were being suppressed in this marriage. I saw how competent, resilient, and brave I really was. I gained a little taste of freedom, being on my own, diving into an activity, working, meeting new people, and all this increased my confidence. Because I got to taste this, it allowed me to be less scared about the possibility of leaving my marriage. Maybe you're reading this and thinking, "I need to get out of my marriage!" If so, what's a small thing you can do that will help you build confidence in yourself to leave? The more you can tap into that zone, the less frightened you'll be to take the leap.

I remember my therapist saying, "You're changing so much, it would take more for you to relate to him now." Instead, I acknowledged how I did feel around him. I felt confused, anxious, filled with self-doubt and constant worry that another women would replace me, and that I was not good enough and not measuring up. These thoughts were not making me feel good! It was time to move on. This relationship was dampening the light inside, the inner voice that I recently started to listen to and the freedom I felt. The aliveness would disappear if I were to continue in this marriage. Weighing the future cost really helped me move on and see what was really true for me. I had outgrown this marriage, and that needed to be honored or else my soul would be in serious danger!

WHAT OPPORTUNITIES ARISE WHEN YOU LEAVE THE MARRIAGE?

Looking at the opportunities of leaving the marriage actually made me feel excited and scared at the same time! When you're looking at the opportunities, what do you see for yourself? Maybe it's diving deeper into passions or discovering new passions. Maybe your passions look like traveling to different places, signing up for a pottery class, learning a new language, or getting more in touch with your body through dance. Maybe it's to learn to go out on your own and eat out enjoying your own company. Maybe it's getting to hang out with liked-minded women who are on similar path of self-discovery. For me, I lived in Costa Rica for three months on my own and went there knowing no one. I know that sounds extreme, but I was really up for the challenge of embracing and learning about the new me. I rode a bike through neighboring towns, stopped at various beaches, talked with complete strangers, and did yoga on the beach. I felt so alive and connected to nature. What adventures and exciting possibilities are waiting for you?

YOUR SIGNS AND SIGNALS SUPPORT YOU

I would receive signs and signals that I was on the right path. I remember doing yoga one morning and coming back to my little cottage on the beach, and these dogs came rushing towards me with wagging tails, licks, and jolly faces. This hit my heartspace and brought me to my knees. I heard a voice say, "One dog was taken away, and I give you three." You see, I lost a dog in my divorce. This experience reignited my heart and also woke me up to the possibility of some greater force guiding my steps. What signs and signals are you receiving to direct you to leave your marriage? They are coming, but you need to pay attention to receive them. When you embrace your signs and signals, a whole world opens up to support your movement. The point of me sharing this with you is that I couldn't have known the sweet things that were waiting for me. I had to trust that something better was in store, and what really happened was a whole other world opened up to me. A world where I get to choose my experiences, I get to exercise my voice, and I get to feel love on the inside and the outside! Where can you open up more so the sweetness of life can direct you with grace?

HAVING YOUR OWN BACK

I know this sounds crazy because I'm telling you to trust in the universe, cut the chord from your parents, and learn to have your own back. Why would you want to do this at a time like this, right!? When my parents were unable to emotionally be there for me in my separation, this was a super pivotal moment. Why? The truth is I was being set up for learning the art of having my own back. If you take one thing away from this book, this is it! Learning to have your own back is the most important thing you can do for yourself. Why? Because there will come a time again in your life where you'll be faced with another challenge. Maybe your parents won't be alive, and if they are, they most likely won't have the skillset to support you in the way you'd like. Isn't it time to set them free of this?

I know it's heartbreaking to read this. But think of it this way: they have certain expectations of you that you can't live up to. It works the other way around. You have things you'd like from them that they're ill equipped to provide to you. Learning the fact that my parents couldn't emotionally support me was so lonely and devastating at first. But it was also freeing. How? Because it woke me up to the fact that I need to learn how to take care of my own emotional support here. I need to learn how to pick myself up when I fall down. Do you see why coming to this realization is a huge part of the puzzle for you?

BUT HOW TO DO IT?

I decided to choose the path of having my own back. So, how exactly did I do it? I found ways to release tension and deal with the uncertainty I was facing. I honed my breathing through yoga. I hiked my butt off, and I meditated. I prayed and asked higher source for answers to guide me. I cried so many nights into my pillow, releasing the toxic emotions I was carrying. What can you do to get yourself started? Please understand, it hurt so much to embrace this reality, yet this is the choice that helped me to step into myself, the new person I was becoming. I learned to release these fears so I could move on and not fight for something that wasn't going to happen. My parents were not capable of giving me what I needed. When I did release the fears, I could see things about myself. For example, how I'd been thinking about leaving this marriage for quite some time, but ran from the thoughts by busying myself. And how it was so easy for me to cope with my fears by pleasing others, collecting things, and seeking approval.

I went to therapy and had loads of discoveries there! I discovered I used to talk to myself harshly, saying things like, "You're stupid," "Why aren't you getting this?" and "I can't believe you did that!" I would create these visceral hateful emotions in my body and couldn't stand myself. To turn this around, I needed to speak more nicely to myself and learn how to have my own back. When I had a hard day or went through something difficult, I'd find ways to shift my mood. I'd take a bath and softly soothe myself saying, "It's okay, I know you had a rough day. You'll get through this. You're amazing. You're going through so many changes all at once, and you're still standing." I learned how to self-soothe, and I didn't need to seek anything from the outside to make me feel better. It's wonderful to have cheerleaders as well, but there's nothing like having your own back. It gives you this self-assurance that no matter what, you're going to be fine! I also shift into gratitude and this helps me hone the gifts I've been given. Like saying I have my health, I'm thankful for the sunshine, I love hearing the birds, I love the greenery, and I'm so thankful for my car.

Self-support is critical to leaving your marriage because there are days you're going to hate yourself, it will be hard to take yourself out in public, be hard to face others, talk to family, and that's when you need to pull out your toolkit of self-soothing. You become agile to deal with the highs and lows that arise when you're leaving a marriage. You can learn to calm yourself down and not seek anything from outside like painkillers, drugs, and alcohol to numb you! I got a lot of practice with self-soothing through my divorce. I was served at work and had to face my husband in court several times. Self-soothing gave me a way to release tension. When you learn to self-soothe, you've found the ultimate fountain of rejuvenation, and it's a hundred percent home-grown within, accessible anytime.

Most importantly, I learned the only person that was holding me back from leaving my marriage was me. I'd been unhappy for years upon years and didn't do anything about it. I complained, argued for more time with my husband, wanted more appreciation and love, but was getting nowhere. I just resigned to ignore the issue and go along with this life I'd chosen. It wasn't until this thinking about leaving my marriage really affected my mental health that I was ready to seek help. I was ready to stop this suffering and feeling so bad and hopeless inside. The lesson that was emerging for me was to have my own back. I also didn't have it in my own marriage! Do you feel like this, too? What are you doing to hold yourself back?

Chapter 5

Your Parents' Past is Buried Treasure!

YOUR FAMILY DYNAMICS

Did you have problems understanding why your parents would say or act a certain way with you? I love my parents, and I wasn't sure why they would make certain choices or decisions. I felt a lot of anger toward them for things in my childhood. Like when they didn't come to see me off to college – my mom was so upset when I applied to a college where I wouldn't live at home. She also said we didn't have money for that college, but I applied anyway because a part of me thought what if, and I was really curious to see what would happen. I was the youngest of three and pushed the envelope a bit more. Would your parents be negative and object to things before hearing your reasons for wanting something? I sure had my dose of this, and it gave me thicker skin.

YOUR PLACE IN THE FAMILY

Where do you fall in your family? Are you the oldest, middle child, only child, maybe you come from a herd like my parents? Whatever the case, that tends to influence how you behave in your family. I want you to take stock of this and see how it plays out in your actions with them. I was the youngest, so I had the whole stereotypical baby sister things: I was spoiled, needed to be looked after, couldn't be involved in the decision making, wasn't taken seriously, had to be watched over all the time, and sort of aimlessly tried things only to fall flat on my face.

But I was also the spirited one, laughing the hardest, sensitive to others feelings, people felt comfortable confiding in me, and I seemed to light up the room with my joy. I can say my heart was fully open and easy to bruise in my sort of nonsense kind of family. Because you're raised in a certain way, you may fall into playing that role. You may be seen as one-dimensional when really you have many beautiful qualities. It's your job to uncover the roles and see how true they are for you.

I was treated like the baby, and my sister acted like my second mother. My parents also put a lot of responsibility on my sister to be my caretaker. Maybe this sounds familiar to you. Maybe you're the one who took care of your little sister. Maybe you helped your mom plan for the prayers, shopped, and helped organize events for the family. Maybe you checked in with your mom about every little decision, like what clothes to buy, what class to take, what to wear. Maybe you're still looking for permission in your adulthood. We get into these patterns and playing roles so early on, it becomes so comfortable to stay in that zone. But you're not just someone's daughter, mother, sister, or daughter-in-law; you are a life with its own set of thoughts, values, insights, and it's your job to write your own story. So, how do you even do that?

First, see where you fall in the line and what family dynamics play out in your own life. By doing this, you'll start putting some pieces of your puzzle together. We all play roles in our family, and this may exist long into our adulthood. By examining this, you can create awareness to start changing your role within your family. For example, because I was the youngest, it was easy for me to go along with my family's decisions. One case, I remember my mom sending my sister to come collect me for an uncle's party. We were all on vacation together, and I didn't feel like attending. I had a long day and didn't want to hang with a boisterous crowd. It would have been fun, but my heart wasn't in it. And in our culture, you're supposed to go to everything and have a good reason if you don't show up. My sister came loudly knocking at my door saying, "Mom said you need to go." Here we were, adult women, and she was playing the role of caretaker. Why? Because this was my mother's wish, and this was tied to my mother not wanting to disappoint her brother who was throwing this bash!

Furthermore, another party was scheduled the next day, so I'd be seeing everyone that I missed the night before. Have you been in this situation? Where you have to answer to an entire crowd for your absence? It can be a little daunting if everyone is looking at you like you abandoned them. Are you seeing how your choice to make a different decision can affect the entire group? This is what happens when you are leaving your marriage. You need to take into account the changes that may happen so you are more equipped to handle them when them arrive at your door.

THE RELATIONSHIP BAR

What kind of relationship do your parents have? My parents had a traditional relationship, and the gender roles were very set for most of my childhood. My mom was a stay-at-home mom and my dad was the breadwinner, traveling for work with a good profession as a chemical engineer. My mom cooked, cleaned, sewed, planned parties, took almost total care of us shopping, cleaning, feeding, and seemed to have a to-do list as long as the Nile river! Does this sound familiar? Maybe you experienced this, and this is your own life now. Maybe you're running pillar to post so the whole family's needs can be taken care of. Think back and see what kind of relationship your parents had. Your parents are the earliest role models you have, and it influences how you look at intimate relationships.

Your parents' relationship sets the bar for your future relationship. How? We go toward what we know. It's our comfort zone. Look closely. Does your spouse have traits like your dad or mom? For me, my husband mirrored my dad pretty well. They were both not able to grasp their emotional life, they were comfortable with putting blame on their spouse, and life centered around them. The way my parents interacted and reacted to one another was surely setting me up for what was deemed acceptable in a relationship. For example, my mom spoke about infidelity and even said dad use to hit her. She would say to my sister and I, "You can't trust men; they cheat." In fact, it seem all the women in my culture felt and carry that fear within them. Can you look back now and see what you may have picked up from your mom and dad's relationship? Maybe some of this is trailing you, wearing you down, and tainting your perception of yourself.

The more I examined my parents relationship, the more I saw similar patterns in my marriage. I also saw how strange my parents' relationship really was. They hardly showed affection to each other, maybe a peck on the cheek and dancing at events. But they didn't greet each at the door, they didn't whisper sweet nothings in each others' ears, they hardly held hands, and didn't have close conversation with each other. For example, they didn't talk about their feelings or hurts with one another. In fact, they used us as a conduit for communicating their feelings. Putting us in the middle, my mom would say, "Ask your father why he's so cheap and doesn't want to go anywhere!" Was this your experience with your parents? I believe the missing parts in my mom's relationship with dad was she couldn't communicate her thoughts, feelings, and emotions to him. He didn't get emotions and he didn't get feelings. She also didn't see her own worthiness and values.

YOUR EMOTIONAL ROLLERCOASTER

How has your parents way of relating affected your emotional life? When my parents fought, they yelled at one another. It was hard for me to open up to them. For example, opening up to my dad was like me putting myself in a war zone. If I opened up to him, this was a path to feeling like a fool, belittled, or crazy for having a feeling. He said things like, "Why are you so moody? What's your problem? Why do you have a sour face?"

I was hit with judgments and assumptions before I could even get a chance to express. Do you know what that feels like? Maybe you do. It retards your ability to process your feelings and work through them. Why? Because you're stuck in avoidance, confusion, guilt, or shame. It's like I was put on trial for having the emotions, so better to hide or not express them at all. My dad was terrible at boundaries with everyone, not just my mom. I remember he would barge into my room anytime he had the impulse. If the door was locked, he would pound it because what he had to convey was more important than anything you were doing. I never could predict what mood they were going to be in, and it seem like they would trigger each other often. Being around them sent me on an emotional rollercoaster of highs and lows. Perhaps you feel like you're not sure what you're stepping into when you interact with your parents. Maybe things are fine, but all of sudden, you're in in the middle of a yelling match! And if you don't move out of the way, you can be taken down, too.

HIDING FROM MY FAMILY

Do you find yourself hiding from your family? Living in this kind of environment made it easy for me to be less transparent with my own feelings. I remember later on in my early teens, I started feeling really embarrassed when my father called me dumb. He was my math tutor, and when I wasn't getting a math problem, he would casually say, "You're so dumb; why aren't you getting this?" Then he would chuckle and this made me feel embarrassed and a little hopeless. I eventually recruited my cousin to tutor me and didn't have to deal with the backlash from my dad. Looking back, this experience really shot my self-confidence. But I surely didn't know that then, and I didn't have the words to communicate that this hurt my feelings. Are you able to voice your concerns with your family? Are you able to make mistakes and learn from them without being judged? Or do you feel like you're tiptoeing and trying to avoid embarrassment? There wasn't room to be soft in my family; we sort of danced around our feelings, and it cost us dearly later on. How? We really struggled when it came to talking about big issues like finances, marriage, college, and places to live. It seemed like a lot of things were being piled on top, and it was just us playing roles reacting to each other. Do you find yourself shaking in your boots when you have to talk to your parents about big issues? Of course, or else you probably wouldn't be reading this book! The point is to acknowledge if you've had to hide and dance around your feelings with your parents. Why? Because this is key to knowing how to navigate your parents.

I couldn't be myself with my parents, but I didn't even know what that meant until leaving my marriage. I was comfortable with hiding stuff from my family, so when my marriage started breaking down I naturally hid that from them because I felt they would be disappointed and frustrated with me. Maybe you've kept your feelings and hurts to yourself for the same reason. Do you find yourself dancing around questions to avoid an interrogation? Do you put up a fake facade to make your parents feel everything is going wonderfully in your life? In my parents eyes, I had a dream marriage with a super successful husband. I'd gotten so good at telling them only the good stuff in our relationship. Is this you? I'd learn things like revealing my frustration, confusion, and pain in my marriage wasn't going to get rewarded by them! Maybe your parents think like this too. The funny thing is, our parents can only give us what they have to give. It's our job to not try to demand something from them that may not be in their capacity to give. It's the same thing as them wanting us to be a certain way for the sake of their own happiness.

I also couldn't communicate with them because I was so confused inside. I hated myself and felt like I wasn't contributing to the relationship. I felt hopeless most of the time and when my ex belittled my accomplishments, harped on me, or said I was a burden, it stung so much because I believed that already for myself. Maybe you felt like me, ashamed, hopeless, and confused. How would you even know where to start telling your parents you were thinking about leaving your marriage? You can't go to opening your heart to your parents if you've been hiding from them most of your life.

INVESTIGATING YOUR LIFE

When my marriage was falling apart, I was trying to do anything to hold it together because I didn't want to bring shame to my family. I felt guilty for not doing better and didn't want to face all the stuff that would come from my big extended family. You're probably thinking, "What will everyone say about me? What will happen to my family's name? I don't want to hurt my parents and make them disappointed in me." Now is the perfect time for you to become investigator of yourself. Get curious about how you got in this situation and why is this happening to you now. I became an investigator and watched my actions and behavior. I was suffering so much in my marriage that I was willing to do anything for me to start feeling better. So I sought out therapy to understand myself more.

In therapy, I first learned that I wasn't so awful; in fact, I was the opposite! I'll never forget the first session my therapist said, "Your husband has been whispering lies in your ears." The statement was so earth shattering because for the very first time in my life, someone was saying the opposite to me. Could it really is true? Could I really have been lied to for so long? And you know what, it didn't stop there because it started with childhood. Have you had that moment where someone's message hits your heartspace and you feel that's your truth? It's like they shine a light, and you see something so real that it's both groundbreaking and scary at the same time.

Therapy also helped me dig into my childhood and uncover little breadcrumbs to help me find my way back to my own truth. I saw how growing up where you were called stupid and dumb, reprimanded, had no privacy set me up to attracted a partner who treated me similarly. For example, in childhood, my mom opened my mail, went through my things, and would also barge into my bedroom.

It also wasn't safe to talk to her about my emotions. I had my first heartbreak, and I remember sitting on my bed and I was so darn sad. She said, "What's wrong with you?" I explained what happened, she looked at me, paused, and then laughed in my face. I was so confused by that reaction. It didn't seem right for what was going on, and I didn't know how to navigate it. She made me feel so uncomfortable. She brushed off her laugh when she saw it was upsetting me more and said, "It's no big deal, you don't have to get so upset." It was such a little moment in my life, but it informed me that it was not safe to share my heart with my family.

I just knew I had to armor up and pretend that things were fine. My emotional part of me was stunted from that experience. When I took the time to study myself, my reactions to people, my hiding from my family, my emotionally unavailable partnership, the patterns emerged so clearly! I encourage you to look at pivotal times in your childhood. How did they play out? What do you remember feeling? How was it handled by your parents? Were you taught to ignore your feelings, brush things off, or downplay your emotions for the sake of others? I know it's uncomfortable to go there sometimes because bringing up past hurts can feel so painful. But looking at the past is also a way of clearing it. Why? Because you acknowledge that it in fact did happen, and you take responsibility for that emotion. Then you make the space to see patterns from your childhood and how it's playing out in your life right now.

IT'S NOT ALL ABOUT YOU

When your parents act out, it's so easy to take it personally. But truthfully, it's not about you. Your parents put their highest hopes and biggest fears they have on you. They want the best for you, but truthfully they may be using fear to do so. They may also have never had a real mom or dad that empowered them and uplifted them. They may have had no parenting at all! Mine didn't because they came from such a large herd and were put to work very early on. Their childhood was stripped, and their own parents had less than that!

For example, telling my parents about my separation and receiving the disappointment from them was tough. In fact, I remember they were angry, saying it's the biggest mistake I'm making. I remember my dad saying this is disappointing, he got hysterical and went into prayer saying, "God, please bless this house and clear whatever darkness has come to plague it." He started crying, shaking, and it took so much out of him. It also took so much out of me to bear witness to this!

Instead of letting this experience swallow me whole, I started getting really curious about why my parents were so darn unsupportive of me leaving my marriage. Maybe you've experienced this level of disappointment from your parents. I encourage you to look back in your life and see why your parents reacted the way they did. Once you open this door, it will lead you to ask questions about their past, and you'll probably learn things about them that will shock you! This will allow you to develop compassion and even forgiveness for their journey. You'll see that their reaction to you is really all about them. They are still holding on to stuff that makes them react a certain way to you. This experience helped me see that I had everyone else's back but not my own. It was time for me to train myself to have my own back.

FINDING YOUR BURIED TREASURE

When you dig into your parents past it's like finding buried treasure. For example, I learned that my mom asked her parents' permission to leave her marriage. It was heartbreaking to hear that they told her, "You are married now, you need to stick with this commitment." The sad thing is that my mom grew up in a very different place and time. She had no job, minimal education, no therapist, no support network, and most of the women were getting physically and emotionally abused.

What have you learned about your parents past that can help you move forward? I learned that my mom stayed in the marriage and locked her heart up so she could survive. She made choices to help her detach from her heart and dove into her role as mother and wife. She was never going to have a self-discovery journey, to talk about her feelings, release, and process them. She was going to solider on and support the family unit at the cost of her soul. Knowing all this, it was easy for me to see why she reacted to my own divorce with disappointment. Do you see where I'm going here? There are clues waiting for you, and you just need to do the work to find them.

LOVING YOUR PARENTS

How can you love your parents? How can you learn to love them even more when you're going through this tough time? By learning how they were as children. My mom is one of twelve and my dad is one of thirteen. They were put to work as little soldiers with chores, had schooling, and helped their parents at work. There was no parents reading bed time stories, talking to them about their feelings, asking them to use their words to communicate instead of acting out, there was no cuddling, and limited parenting. Did your parents have a similar upbringing? My mom told me that my dad used to get beaten so much for acting out, she said he was beaten so badly once and not given food. She said she was beaten by her own older brother when she acted out. There was no such thing as having a temper tantrum. All of this made me see the scared little boy and girl in my parents. I could see now when they act out with me being judgmental, angry, and harsh with their words, intimidating, this was all they knew.

This made me realize that asking for their support was going to be a stretch for them. How could they give me something that they didn't have to give? I had to adjust my expectations of their ability to emotionally support me because it just wasn't in them. It's not fair for me to have these expectations of them because, in a way, it's the same thing as them expecting me to be a certain way. Maybe you need to examine your expectations of your parents. Maybe they are set too high, and that's why you keep getting disappointed. Maybe if you tweak them a bit, you'd create the space for something different to happen. Perhaps you feel like it's been two sides pushing against each other, and nothing gets solved. You're right because this strategy causes more friction, more distance, more heartache, and more loneliness.

I've learned to do something different. I wanted to understand, get curious, and see how I could rise above this dynamic. Do you want that, too? I also think that was part of my learning as I grew into adulthood. When you take the time to learn about yourself and your parents, it creates the space for you all to relate in a possibly different way. I was feeling more confident in myself. I was able to speak my truth with them and become less and less bothered by their reactions. This was different for them. They were seeing me in a new way, and it allowed them to soften up a bit and treat me with more openness. What was I doing? I was modeling a way for them to treat me. I was teaching them how I would like to be treated. And by adopting compassion toward my parents and their journey, this helped me grow into myself. Do you know that quote by Gandhi, "Be the change you wish to see?" This is what was happening between me and my parents. I invite you to think about this possibility for yourself. It can be done, but first you need to examine yourself and your parent's background.

YOUR PARENTS' HIGHEST HOPES

Remember how I said your parents put their highest hopes and biggest fears on you at the same time? Their highest hopes for you can be this marriage. You're their crown and glory. They are looking for you to fulfill their hopes. In a way, your marriage was their dream, too.

What do I mean? They took the plunge with you and have probably been on this marriage journey with you. For example, my parents invested money, they invested time, commitment, and they even traveled to India to me my husband's family. Our families went on trips together, and it was truly marrying a family also. They were proud to talk about me to their siblings. In a way, they were living through my life. They also were forming bonds with my husband's family. Do you see how this intertwinedness they feel can disrupt them, too? In a strange way, you leaving this marriage can mean their heart is being broken, too. I hope this helps shift some things for you and gives you a higher perspective here!

REWRITING YOUR STORY WITH YOUR PARENTS

How do you rewrite the story with your parents? If I was going to be writing my story, I had to do it slowly and with complete awareness because I had operated from the latter for most of my life! I started changing my roles with them slowly. It came out by me telling them less about my decisions about the marriage. I told them less about my finances, and I got pretty good at figuring out what felt right to tell them and what seemed like an invasion of my privacy. For example, I remember my mom asking how often I was having sex with my husband? That was clearly crossing boundaries there! I remember my mom giving me negotiating advice: "Don't take too much from him." Does this make sense? What things do your parents ask you that seem like they shouldn't be privy to that information? You have to figure out what is out of bounds in order to know where to set your boundaries.

BEFRIEND HEALTHY BOUNDARIES

Since I had really poor boundaries with my parents, this needed to change in order to rewrite our story! With practice, it became easier for me to set and enforce healthy boundaries with my parents. In fact, having healthy boundaries is one of the secrets to leaving your marriage successfully! Here you get to be intentional, measure what's right/not right for you, and how to enforce it when boundaries are crossed. This clears any monotonous back and forth that makes the whole process wishy-washy. Example: when my parents asked how my finances are, I say, "I know you love and care for me, but know that's not up for discussion, and I'm doing fine." I then redirect the conversation to things we can enjoy talking about, common interests, issues going on in the world, and home improvements! What do you think about this approach? Perhaps it may seem scary at first, but that is the very reason why it needs to be done. Setting healthy boundaries allows you to feel safe and protected in the same space with others. You also give your parents a chance to learn how you'd like to be treated by modeling what is okay and what is not okay. Start with small things, and do it slowly.

Enforcing boundaries has allowed me to also love my parents even more. I get respect from them, and I show my love and respect for them. It's not something I perfected overnight. In fact, I still struggle to talk with my parents at times, and that's when I hit the pause button until I feel my best. When I feel my best, I'm able to show up fully and hold the space for whatever shows up with them. How do you want to show up with your parents? How do you want to feel in their presence? How do you want them to treat you?

HEALING YOUR PARENTAL BONDS

I'm falling more and more in love with my parents. I love all their quirks, silly antics, crazy talk, and I just plain love them. I think they feel like they can be more themselves and it lets them release the "parenting role" and communicate with me from a different place. One of my favorite memories with them is walking on Cannon beach in Oregon and taking in the sunset. It was their first time doing this, and looking at them, I got to see them like a child taking in something new with brightness, play, and wonderment. Can you see the little boy and girl in your parents? For me, I love seeing when this comes out.

The walk on the beach was beautiful; it was like God commanding that whole trip of healing. Why? Prior to this trip, we talked about how they handled the news of my divorce and what they could have done differently. I had opened the conversation by saying, " I would love for them to show up to support me in my divorce." I pointed out with love and care what they did and what I would have liked to see. But I did it in a way that wanted to heal and grow the bonds with them. I said, "I want to get closer to you you'll so we need to clear the air about something." They said they were sorry and also sent me a lovely note and care package. This was a big gesture from my parents. I honored that and was grateful for it. Our relationship had grown, and they were in a space where I could confide in them. Knowing when the time is right to confide in your parents is key. There needs to be an openness in you, a non-attachment to their reactions, trust, and a processing of your own hurts.

I knew something bigger was unfolding in our relationship. They were seeing someone who had grown, someone to be taking seriously, and who was capable of stepping into her own. I was feeling more and more comfortable with myself and what I stood for. This was radiating out, and I was attracting a different kind of relationship with my parents. Also, being able to be yourself and share your heart with your parents is an amazing gift. I invite you to engage in the possibilities of creating a different kind of relationship with your parents.

Chapter 6

Conscious Uncoupling

UNCOVER YOUR REAL INTENTION

What's your underlying bedrock intention for leaving this marriage? When you uncover that, it's going to be key to helping you leaving this marriage. Getting really clear about the why of why you're doing this will help you navigate the waters ahead. Make no mistake, these waters will be of different scales – rough with torrential downpours, choppy waves with snowcap tips, and fog where you can't see where the shore is! But there will also be moments where you get a glimmer of the moonlight, you look up to see the patterns in the stars, and you sigh in relief for how far you've come. But before you can experience all these wonders, you need to get clear about your intention. This will also sustain you and give you fuel for what's to come. My dear, in order to get even close to your "why," you have to be willing to do a few things first.

CUT YOUR EXTERNAL NOISE

First, you have to be willing to cut the external noises and make space for yourself. This is not always easy to do with having a demanding family, in-laws, kids, demands from social circles, and friends. You will be getting guidance from everyone even if you didn't ask for their input. There are people like your parents who all have their best intentions for you, but at the end of the day it is still "their" intentions for you, not yours. This is why you can't be clouded by this, and how you do this is by making the space for yourself.

Another key to leaving a marriage is the ability to listen to that inner voice I spoke about earlier. It's your map, your compass, your North Star, the divine, your God, whatever you call it… get in touch with it. I hear this voice mostly when I'm alone. For me, this happens when I go into nature. Staring up at the blue sky and white clouds, looking up at trees towering over me with their trunks sprawling up and open towards the sun. I take in intricate patterns on the backs of the leaves, the water veins, and I see how detailed and organized life is! I see how resilient and sustainable it is. I see how a gentle breeze moves things up and down with no effort. Mother nature has taught me to be gentle, and I've become more present by just taking in her natural beauty. It's like time stops, and I'm taken to a depth within myself that is timeless and dimensionless. Here in this space, I'm able to connect to my heartspace, what's important to me, what I value, and which direction is right for me. Here I'm able to rise above the muck of what life threw me. Bill Gates says he takes two weeks off, and he calls this his think weeks! Here he gets to see what's important and think through his plans and decisions. I encourage you to take this time for yourself. Of course, it doesn't have to be two weeks; you can certainly start anywhere! I encourage you to start small and start soon.

I've learned to cut the noise in order to make some of the biggest decisions of my life. I've adopted this in my schedule as a regular thing, practicing this daily and on longer periods with harder decisions.

CARVING OUT TIME

Now I know what you're thinking. *How am I going to find the time for myself?* If you don't do this, you won't uncover what is true for you. You won't be able to navigate the things ahead with more ease and clarity. The better question *is how can I afford not to do this?* Think of giving this as a gift to yourself so you show up better for yourself and others in the world. You become more yourself when you spend time getting to know "you" and how you operate and what you value. It doesn't happen with others and by others telling you who you are. That stuff can change, and then it's creating a dependency to seek outside yourself for answers. Only you know the best answer for yourself, but you have to be willing to hone this skill! Of course, there are amazing mentors, coaches, and role models who can bring out and inspire wonderful things within you, but at the end of the day, you are the one doing the heavy lifting. It starts with doing the groundwork yourself.

YOUR INTUITION GUIDES YOU

The heavy lifting comes from you, and when you are alone and get quiet, you can tap into your intuition. You have a beautiful heart that guides you. It alerts you and talks in signs, signals, fear, pain, suffering, sickness, in whispers and eventually loud thumps over the head when you really need to hear something! The key is paying attention to these prompts because they're trying to navigate you to a higher way of being.

Besides communing with nature, another way I tap into my heartspace is through meditation. Sitting quietly, I focus on my breath, inhaling and exhaling slowing in and out of my nostrils. I think of my belly expanding out like a balloon on the inhale and then contracting slowly on the exhale. I place one hand on my heart, and this simple act starts to make me feel more grounded, aware, and tapped into my heart. Did you know that we have a brain in our heart? According to Heartmath LLC, they discovered that we have a little brain in our heart. We have forty thousand neurons located in our heart that can sense, learn, and feel! The say our heart can speak to and influence the brain. Why is this important? Being able to tap into your heartspace helps you know what decision is right or not right for you. That's where you get to meet that future self that is trying to guide you to a higher way of being. It's your intuition, higher self, source, God – whatever you call it, it's your key to liberation.

WRITING TO YOUR HIGHER SELF

Another example of connecting to my higher self is through writing. I've been keeping a journal since 2006! Here, I would write my thoughts, feelings, and emotions, and this process has evolved over the years. This helps me clear the clutter from my mind to really see what's true for me. Do you keep a journal? I encourage you to keep a daily journal writing your heart away and allowing it to flow freely. Write whatever comes up for you uncensored. It's a place to collect your thoughts. It's your private doorway into what you're feeling, and you'll even discover things that are hidden. The more you do this practice, your answers will come more clearly and more quickly. For me, my heart starts answering back to me on the page because I've been doing this practice frequently and for such a long time. I'm blessed to have access to this tool because it's helped me tap into my intuition and can be a great tension release!

BLOOM YOUR BEST SELF

How do you bloom your best self? What does that even mean? It's like crafting your own personal mission statement. It can be one sentence, a word, phrase, a list of things and it has to have meaning for you. Mine looks like this:

- I am the creator of my life
- I connect with my God
- I make time to dream
- I trust myself
- I serve with heart
- I show compassion to all
- I forgive and let go
- I do more of what I love
- I manage my time and energy
- I am honest and walk in the space of vulnerability
- I play and create!

This is vital to helping you navigate, keeping you on track, and helping you to strive to become a better version of yourself. Here you're looking for your values, gifts, and ethics. All this helps you see more of your inner strength and inner beauty. Also, ask yourself questions like who do you want to be? What do you want to do with your life? Who are your role models in life? What traits do they have that you like? When you overcame a big goal, what traits came out of you to do so? What did you learn about yourself during that time? I suggest taking all this information and crafting a personal mission statement. This exercise helps you to self-reflect, identify your strengths, and see where you'd like to go!

There will even be a pattern of your positive traits that is echoed back to you from your cheerleader family members, friends, and network. You have to do the digging to uncover this for yourself. I remember when I was leaving my marriage, one of my biggest supporters and advocates happened to be my boss. She would point out what a good job I was doing, what colleagues were saying about me, she shared my review where folks chimed in unanimously about how positive I was, I was a team player, friendly, easy to talk to, smart, fun to be around, grounded in tough situations! These comments were so shocking for me to see. But there it was, the words staring me in the face from people who had worked very closely with me on long and arduous projects. This also made me learn the important distinction between surrounding yourself with cheerleaders versus emotional vampires. More on that in chapter 9!

Doing the work to spend time alone, tap into your intuition, craft your mission statement, and consistently do this with discipline helps reveal the parts of you that have been hidden from "You." All these nuggets are what help you combat self-doubt, lack of confidence, feeling too paralyzed to take a step, and feeling unsure of your next step. It builds your inner-strength muscles.

YOU'RE HERE FOR A BIGGER PURPOSE

This also opens the doorway to revealing how much you matter in this world! How your mere presence has the ability to change lives and inspire others. I believe everyone is born with a special purpose to fulfill. No one can do things quite like me, and my gifts are unique to me. Just like your gifts are unique to you, and you came here for a special purpose. I believe it is your job to unearth your gifts so you can get to fulfill your greater purpose. Now, I'm not saying it wasn't your purpose to be a wonderful mother, daughter, daughter-in-law, etc. What I am pointing out is that when something has ended, it's our job to honor that and move on with grace to our next calling so that we may fulfill that bigger purpose. This doesn't mean you devalue your past contributions or demean your past roles. It means a shifting of focus on something that is next in line for you so that your talents and gifts get expressed. These expressions go on to help humanity on a greater scale. For example, if I didn't have the courage to leave my marriage and go through the hero's journey, I wouldn't have had the privilege of connecting and guiding you through this book!

I'm asking you to step outside yourself and see how is leaving your marriage linked to a bigger purpose for yourself. Taking time to honor this huge question may lead to more insight for you. Maybe you already know you're supposed to be doing something different. Maybe it's to start a business, travel the world, learn a new language, work with youth, and go meditate in an ashram. I remember doing a yoga teacher training program when I was going through my divorce. It gave me something to look forward to, I met new friends, and I got attuned with my mind/body. I remember thinking that I'd like to do something in health/wellness down the line. I'm not sure what that looks like as my life is changing so much now, but at least I'm moving toward something that feels right. The rest will come in to focus when the time is right. The point is having this grander vision will help you move forward and give you the added momentum to take that right next step. So do the work to move forward. You are so worth it, and who knows what you'll discover about yourself!

PROTECT YOUR "WHY"

When you've uncovered that "why," hold on to it, protect it, and guard it at all costs! This can mean you want more freedom, more independence. You want to feel less burdened. You want to be happy. You want to find real love and partnership. You want to build inner confidence. For me, it was that I wanted to see if I could be alone and support myself emotionally and financially. I had never seen the women do this in my culture, so this would be my legacy to myself and to help other women find this freedom for themselves. Whatever is revealed for you, honor it. This is your fuel to sustain you in the long road ahead. Leaving a marriage is a big step, and it needs to be honored and done with clarity.

Also keep your why in a place you can see every day, this will be your daily reminder of why this needs to happen. When you focus on it with intention and frequency, it will become your normal. Doing this practice is also setting you up for making more intentional choices and using your time intentionally. It will spill out in other areas of your life, not just leaving your marriage. This means you are transforming, not changing. Indian mystic Sadhguru says the difference between a change and transformation is this: change, you are making a shift in something whereas a transformation means you are burning out everything old to reveal something new. This is music to my ears because that is what is happening here. You are stepping into a new way of being my friend.

By doing all this work, you are seeing who you are and who you'd like to become. This chapter is giving you the tools in order to bridge this gap. You'll probably be amazed at some of the wonderful things you find out about yourself. I found it was a great way to get a higher perspective about myself, how I operate, and where I'd like to go. Now we'll take all this wonderful stuff you're learning about yourself and dive even more into your future self in the next chapter!

Chapter 7

Envisioning – What Amazing Things Manifest When You've Left the Marriage?

SEEING INTO YOUR FUTURE TO COMBAT UNCERTAINTY

Envisioning leaving the marriage and the benefits you gain will help you deal with the uncertainty that comes up during this time. When you're contemplating divorce, there are a lot of unknowns, a lot of scary thoughts coming up, and you get paralyzed from making a decision. Envisioning helps show you ways to break free from that. Remember back in your childhood or even when you spent time with kids how incredibility powerful their imagination is? They could create worlds filled with all sorts of details, touching all the senses. For example, it could be they're living in the castle, they're slaying the dragon, and they have this mighty sword and this magnificent shield that was designed by the village wizard and they just get so delighted in telling you the story! Kids can access their imaginary world immediately and it doesn't matter where they are! This will come in handy when you start do the work of envisioning leaving the marriage. We're going to break apart how to actually do this, how to do it effectively, and how to have it work for you.

CREATE SPACE FOR ENVISIONING

So first you have to create the space for envisioning leaving the marriage. This needs to be physical space, mental space, and blocks of time that you do this. Put it into that schedule you're building for yourself. Envisioning can be done when you're sitting on a bench in a park, going to visit the woods, sitting by river, a lake, a beach, sitting on your patio, or in your prayer room. The area needs to be quiet, and a safe vessel for birthing this vision.

YOUR HEART AND BODY CONNECTION!

The next step to envisioning is to tap into your heart and body to bring out the vision. So we've been talking a lot about accessing the body and the heartspace, and the importance of that is it's the ability for you to feel the emotions and line up your thoughts to produce the feelings within! You can add words of affirmation to this like,

"I feel so much love, I love my surroundings, I'm in this sacred space, and I feel so blessed."

Studying yoga helped me dive deep into understanding and using the chakra system to help me connect to my body and heart. What I learned is you can really access your chakras so they work for you and support this envisioning. If you align the lower chakras with the upper chakras, you can feel the richness of your visions. The lower chakras are controlling basic and emotional well-being. The upper chakras are controlling your thinking centers, your ability to tap into your intuition, to feel clarity. In my marriage, I could not access my lower chakras because I was moving from survival mode. I felt my basic needs weren't getting met. It's only when I developed self-support was I able to access my upper chakras. When I learned to tap into my heart, voice, and intuition, I saw how it all worked beautifully together. You get lovely insight when everything is lined up and you feel the presence of the divine. For example, when you can access your emotions and align it with your thoughts, then you can produce the feelings you want. You can add affirmations using your throat chakra to enhance the richness of this experience.

ENVISIONING EXERCISE

Try this exercise to envision this future for yourself. Sit quietly, close your eyes, and breathe in and out through your nose. On the inhale, your belly should go out like a balloon. On the exhale, pull your belly inward. Do this slowly for ten rounds and place your right hand on your heartspace. Next, visualize a place where you see your future self. She's asked you to come join her and hold space with her. Now, see where she's brought you and take in all the things around you. What are you doing? What are you feeling? How do feel seeing her? Take her in, and using one word, what does she stand for? What benefits are you receiving? Your heart should start communicating with you, leading you through this experience.

Envisioning allows you to get in that sweet spot where the divine inside you lives. You feel grounded, love, supported, like your body is floating. You're vibrating and being wrapped in a bubble of love. Envisioning allows your character traits to come out, and even digs up ones you buried a long time ago. Perhaps you envisioned pursuing a degree, living in a different state/country, learning a new language, and building a school, working with women in domestic violence, or educating children on healthy eating. Whatever is buried in there will come out when you envision. I want you to take the lid off your dreams, dream big, and envision the outcome beforehand. When you think from the end, it's like you're already doing things. When it happens for you, you're already comfortable with it. You welcome it because you've already felt it inside. Adopt this practice and you can continue to expand on your visions. You'll start to see pieces of a puzzle coming together all to support your higher self.

MY OWN ENVISION STORY

I remember when I had this vision to live in another country on my own. One of my cultural taboos was women can't live alone, travel alone, it's not safe, and they're not competent enough to navigate their way. I really had to let go of that stuff! I had tested the waters in small ways to get out of my comfort zone and this was going to be a big leap for me, so I've worked my way up to this. I said, "Ok, let's challenge this cultural belief!" So, living in Costa Rica and not even visiting the town beforehand, I just said, "This is where I'm supposed to go." I was very scared to do this and even freaked out.

I worked with a coach to help me take small steps towards leaving New York. This was getting rid of my apartment in New York City, getting rid of my car, letting go of stuff that I had in my marriage. This was going to be taking me to what was my new chapter, and I had to trust the process. A huge part of what got me through that is envisioning what that would look like for myself.

My coach said, "Do you remember what happened when you left your marriage?" I said, "Colors suddenly came in my life; it was filled with being alive and vibrant."

She said, "What do you think will happen when you take the leap?"

This is what I needed to hear and I started to take steps to leave! One step was writing a letter to my car to support me in this grand vision. Why? My car was nice, my buddy, my safety net, took me places during my divorce, and it was time to part with it, and an amazing thing happened!

CAR TALK

My coach gave me an assignment to write a letter saying goodbye to my car. I didn't feel any major attachment to it, but yet something was holding me back from releasing it. And when I did this assignment, the strangest thing happened. The car started talking to me in this letter, it was like the car writing the letter to me! What it said was, "it's time to let me go, I've served you and you need to go have different rides. But most importantly you have all different adventures in store for you and part of this process is letting me go." I had a nickname for my car called "Mini" because it was a Mini Cooper. Suddenly, Mini was giving me words of wisdom so I could move towards my vision! My Mini was right, because I had many different rides. I rode on boats, bicycles, carts, trains, horses, and planes! I'm sharing this because when you make the time to envision, miraculous things happen. When you get to clear the clutter of the noise from the external world, you really see that you're on the right path for yourself.

GET CREATIVE TO ENHANCE YOUR ENVISIONING SKILLS!

Another way to solidify and expand your envisioning skills is to do creative activities. I love free dancing, moving my body into different positions, this opens up something for me. Another one is water coloring! I had a really wonderful, dear friend who is an artist and she shared her knowledge of water coloring. I noticed how it really allowed me to see my patterns. For example, I wasn't going out of the border of the page when I was painting. I was using the same stroke and she said, "Oh, you can play around and get messy!" She showed me that I could paint over things, do different shapes, depths, move the paper around so the watercolor would free flow where it wants to on the page. I saw how I approached the water coloring had mirrored my life. I didn't go out of the lines, played it safe, scared to make a mistake, and took it very slowly. This reminded me of how I didn't want to rock the boat in my marriage and how I didn't want to upset my parents, so never told them what was going on in my marriage. Creative actives were helping me collect information about how I operate, and the clearer I got the better I could envision possibilities for myself!

Another activity was yoga, and I was grateful to study it in India and New York. Through yoga, I learned meditation, which helped me become aware of my thoughts. I used breathing to start expanding the space between my thoughts. I could also use visualization. One example is visualizing a big ball of orange light coming towards me, and it's expanding into a huge bubble that engulfs me. Then, I can take any negative thoughts, worries, and fears and put it in this orange bubble. Then I shrink that bubble into the size of a pea, I see a hand coming towards me. It gently held my face saying, "I've got you." It opens its palm towards me and I place this orange ball of light into it. It slowly goes away into the clouds, and I feel a lightness come over me.

Creative activities get you in touch with that side of your brain that can access your vision and expand it. I encourage you to explore activities that you would be attracted to, that maybe you thought you'd like to try. I would come up with a list of creative activities and get your toes wet! Does this sound scary? If so, invite a friend and this may relieve any tension that may arise with you trying something new. The point is to start somewhere and start now!

ENVISIONING 101

How do you start the envisioning process? Here are some general tips. You want to feel your best and your energy level should be up. Think of your energy as a scale from one being low to ten being high. If you're below a five, you probably want to rest, relax, treat yourself nicely, and being kind to yourself. Get it up above a five and then you can start the process. Perhaps that means taking a nice bath, having a healthy dinner, getting a massage, or whatever it takes for you. Just get yourself in that feel good zone for envisioning. Another way to get into that envisioning zone is by being grateful for the things you already have – little things and big things. Maybe it's someone saying hi to you, or perhaps you had a wonderful cup of tea, heard a lovely bird song, or had an amazing nature walk. All those moments are beautiful gifts, and acknowledging this can set you up for envisioning.

If you're having a tough time being grateful, then instead look for the opportunity in the challenges. What is this challenge here to teach you about yourself? What are you learning, because something is emerging and you need to get it. If you don't get it, it's going to come back around because you really need to heighten those awareness centers and enhance your perception. So then when you see the opportunities in the challenges then they don't become so daunting because you've reframed the challenge to serve you. And here, you get closer to being in that feeling good, closer to that five to ten scale of where you can envision. Envisioning requires that you're in a good mental state, physical state, your energy levels are up, your emotional well-being is wonderful, and you're connected to that heartspace! I'm not saying that you're going to feel like this all the time or that this stuff is easy to do. I'm just giving you some tidbits that will help guide you into the envisioning process.

Envisioning is also a good tool to use beforehand with any difficult conversations. For example, if you plan on having a difficult talk with your partner, you can envision the outcome you'd like to see. I've worked with clients where they were scared to say that they wanted to leave their marriage to their partner, so they envisioned the entire conversation beforehand. Specifically, they put the partner in front of them, tell them they want to leave the marriage, and take in the partner's response. Their partner's body could become tight, they could get up and pace the room, and they could feel agitated. I then have them respond to their partner's behavior. My client's response could be just saying, "I see your hurt, I see your face," or it could be very detailed. That way, when they have the real conversation, it's like they've lived it already. Furthermore, when they're ready to have that conversation it's not so daunting because they're prepared. That is the beauty!

Chapter 8

Preparing to Leave – Transition Mojo, Five Biggest Mistakes, and Holiday Blues

YOUR TRANSITION MOJO

Another key to leaving your marriage is developing confidence and resilience to sustain you in your decision. There are times where you're going to be shaken and it's going to be hard, and you're going to want to give up. But if you've developed the confidence, if you're stepping out, if you're doing the work, then you're building that resilience to keep you in "transition mojo." This is like you're birthing something, and you know when you're birthing something, you need focus, discipline, will and a level of trust to take the leap! You're shedding the old you, and you're giving life to something. The same thing is happening here! You're becoming a new you, and all that past stuff is dissolving. That's why preparing to leave needs to be honored, because it's such a big change that you can be hijacked by your body, mind, emotions, and feelings. If you're not vigilant and watching what's happening in your "inside world," then you can be thrown off and give up!

How do we do this? Well, we develop a schedule that is disciplined, it's got frequency to it, and it works for you. And it's got to be things that inspire you to show up. So carve out some time and start putting together a schedule. My schedule looks something like this, and it seemed overwhelming at first! This was developed over time as I figured out what works to help me stay centered and feeling like my best self! I'm not suggesting you use this, because you have to find what works for you. Why? Because you're most likely to stick with it. This should be treated as reference guide.

Time	Monday	Tuesday	Wednes-day	Thurs-day	Friday	Saturday	Sunday
Morning	1 hr Gym+ 15min Medita-tion	1 hr Gym+ 15min Medita-tion	Yoga +30 medita-tion	15min Journal + medi-tation	Yoga+ 30 medi-tation	Outdoor Hike	Yoga-1 hour medita-tion
Daytime	Work	Work	Work	Work	Work ½ day		Work ½ day
Late After-noon	15 Nap		15 Nap			30 Nap	Outdoor Hike
Evening	Outdoor Evening Walk	Outdoor Evening Walk	Outdoor Evening Walk	Outdoor Evening Walk			

Tapping into your heartspace, it means diving deeper and doing that prep work from the earlier chapter. Here, look at your positive traits/qualities, look at the contributions you made in the marriage. Look at the time effort and how you showed up! This could mean your hopes for the family, organizing the parties, looking after your sick kids, shuffling them to play dates, giving your kids pep talks because they are being bullied as school, looking after the plants, picking out the curtains, taking care of your in-laws, organizing religious events, being there to cuddle with them, doing the laundry, being a tour guide, decorator, admin for the household. All these things need to be honored and valued. I used to undercut my contributions and see them as "little things." But they weren't, these things contributed to the family and a sense of home. All that stuff is really beautiful, and you were there to do it! Listing your contributions allows you to see and acknowledge how you show up in this marriage. It's going to do something internally for you when times get tough, it will also expand your confidence.

GETTING PHYSICAL!

What does this mean? It means get your butt moving. Another step for leaving the marriage is to make space to get in touch with your body through physical activity. This can be walking, yoga, running, stretching, breathing, hiking, swimming, dancing, meditating, and much more. Our body stores emotions and this can be an emotional time. Our body is also made up of so much memory, and through my own experiences, I learned how it was vital to release heavy emotions. This can build up in the body making us feel heavy, weighted down, and this stuff needs to be flushed out of our system often. Also, our mind holds memory, but think about all those cells in your body and what they're carrying! Our body has more memory than our mind!

When you physically connect to your body, you're able to tap into the signals/feedback that it's sending to you. You can feel it, sense it, and see its warning signs very early on. Listening to warning signals helps you navigate, and it can come in the form of a pain in the neck, weird anxious feeling in your gut, hairs standing up on your arm, or funny feeling that something is not quite right. Listen to those the first time, and you'll save yourself a lot of heartache/sickness early on.

When you're contemplating divorce, there are so many highs and lows. Tapping into the body and communicating with it will help you navigate this time.

In my yoga teacher-training program, I was breathing, stretching, bending, twisting, and it really opened up deeper dimensions within me. I became more attuned, sensitive and my body awareness increased. For example, I could sense my feelings quicker, make sense of them, and know how to self-correct in order to feel rejuvenated.

What a wonderful tool to heighten your senses, become more grounded, release tension, and hit the reset button – I highly recommend it!

WRITING TO YOUR HEART

Another concrete way to deal with the highs and lows in divorce is through writing. Since 2006, I've kept a journal, writing down my thoughts, feelings, and emotions. I started by following Julia Cameron's method from *The Artist's Way*, called the morning pages. She suggests writing three pages or fifteen minutes every day, simply dumping any thoughts on the page. You don't censor, judge, clean up the thoughts… it's totally free writing and for your eyes only. This is an amazing tool for when you're thinking about divorce because it helps you release tension, have a place to put stuff so it's not stuck in your body, and also go back to it for self-refection.

I also keep a gratitude journal where I write down five things I'm so grateful for that day. Some days are harder than others, but there's always something to be grateful for if you look hard enough. And if you can't bring yourself to do a gratitude journal, then start reframing your challenges about leaving this marriage. Look at them as *what are the opportunities sprouting up here that I can learn from, that I can use later for the future to make me a better person?* All of these options are so powerful and put you in that space of building confidence and resilience!

RIDING A BIKE FOR THE FIRST TIME

When you start implementing these tools, it is going to feel weird, especially if you haven't done something like this. The key is to start simple by picking a couple things to implement into your schedule and picking times of the day that you know you can consistently block out that time. Monitor the frequency of your activities. For example, if you're writing in your journal two days a week and still feeling like it's not doing anything, tweak the frequency. Try it four days a week. Evening walks in nature is a great way because you get to observe nature and let your stress melt away. Pick activities you want to do, and do this stuff alone, because you're getting in touch with that inner space.

FIVE BIGGEST MISTAKES WOMEN MAKE
Being Alone

I'm going to share my five biggest mistakes that women make when they are thinking about leaving their marriage. The first is not being able to spend time alone. Not being able to enjoy your own company alone is a crime. This can be eating a meal alone, going for a walk alone, book a day trip all to yourself. I know that may sound weird to you. Especially if you've been taught to fill your schedule and take care of everyone else's needs! I always was running from pillar to post and I didn't have time to be alone. I didn't want to be alone and face my thoughts.

But when you spend time alone, you get to take stock of your own body, mind, and heartspace without interruption. This is a sacred time and you're opening up the challenges of communication with yourself. Also if you don't spend time alone, you can become a slave to people because your energy is going completely towards them! Giving your energy entirely to others can become draining, and you will surely not be able to reach clarity for yourself during this time. You are leaving no time to see what your heart wants, face any negative thoughts, and look at any unexamined perceptions you hold for yourself. You're also not giving yourself a chance to create your own identity. Your own likes, dislikes, and discoveries. Do you feel like it's awkward to spend time alone? If so, you'll need to start small. When you are brave enough to be alone, then you can address negative thoughts using some of the tools I mentioned: writing, breathing, stretching, tapping into your heart, going into nature...these are all a remedy for some of that stuff.

Headtrash: Those Creepy Gremlins

Another big mistake women make when contemplating divorce is falling victim to their headtrash – AKA their gremlins. These are the negative stories looping in your mind. It could look like, "I'm not good enough, I don't deserve this, who am I? I don't want this for myself, I'm being selfish, I am ugly, it's not worth the trouble, I don't want to rock the boat, I feel like I don't matter, what's the point? I feel like no one listens to me, I feel incapable of managing my life, I feel worthless." Headtrash keeps you stuck because it keeps playing and playing, and it's not being addressed. This culprit affects your behavior and you can't even access it sometimes because you've buried so much on top of it! But all of it must be looked at in order for you to leave this marriage with confidence and take big leaps for yourself.

Okay so how do you solve this headtrash problem? Spend time alone to hear it, to create space between your thoughts, examining where the thoughts came from, and then embracing/creating new neural pathways for yourself. It takes an average of sixty-six days to form a new habit, according to the European Journal of Social Psychology.

For example, if you talk to yourself in a harsh way, maybe you're beating yourself up; the key is to catch yourself doing it by expanding the space between your thoughts. You can put your awareness on your breath, body, surroundings, go into nature, do an action like making a cup of tea. Then *bam!* You've opened the doorway to break this cycle.

You have to be aware that you're doing in order to self-correct and choose a different thought. When you can separate between you and your thoughts, it changes the way you see yourself! It's your choice to expand that space between your thoughts. Then you can say, "Okay, how is me saying, "I'm terrible!" helping me here? It's not, so instead, I'm going to look at this mistake as I'm in the learning process, or this is how much I know for now, and I'm not going to attach it to my worthiness! You can also replace the thought with something you were proud of that day. "I really have beautiful eyes, I really like my smile, I had a glow, I do see that, I do feel that I made the best dish today and it tasted good, I was focused, this party went off well, you know I had so much planning I paid attention to details, I put out fires at work, I'm such an amazing host, I was showing up and being nurturing and compassionate."

When you connect to this "feel good" zone, I call it being in your sweet spot. We were born to live in this sweet spot. Your inner light shines, and when you can take stock of that, when you can claim it, it actually expands and it becomes your way of being! You feel your body buzzing, your eyes are bright, and you know the truth of who you are so you begin to need less and less validation from the outside world. The outside is attracted to you because you are glowing, but really you're vibrating outward what is already inside you. Another way of letting go of the headtrash is to celebrate your big and small victories! When you've accomplished something, celebrate immediately! It reinforces this loveliness about yourself, and it's going to communicate to your brain these amazing qualities. You're building new neural pathways for yourself. Why? Because you are being a witness to your greatness.

When Did Those Gremlins Hop A Ride?

Another way of letting go of head trash is looking at your past to see where that headtrash comes from. When did you start hearing those things? When did you start saying those things to yourself? When did that become your primary inner dialogue? Because I find they're critical moments in my childhood that formed some of those gremlins. One example is when my dad said, "You're so dumb, you can't figure out this math problem." I began thinking I wasn't the sharpest tool in the shed. I struggled with math and anything math-related. Another example is my mom calling me selfish. I was selfish if I didn't spend time enough time with her. I was selfish if I included her in something or if I wasn't considering her needs in front of my own. To break this cycle, you need to examine your own gremlins and learn to rewrite your story to bring out that lovely light inside.

Afraid to Stand Alone

Are you afraid to stand alone? I'm not talking about being alone, but standing alone when you believe something to be truth for yourself. Another big mistake women make when they want to leave a marriage is not being able to stand-alone. Standing alone is when you come up against challenges from outside authority. This can be your parents, extended family, or social circles. They may be all chanting, "You're making a big mistake here!" I remember when I was contemplating divorce, I told an aunt and her advice was to stay in the marriage. She said, "If your husband is not beating you, you should stay with him. He's taking care of you." That was her checklist for a good partnership.

Instead of getting mad at this reaction, I got curious with her. I asked her why she thought that, and then she said, "I married your uncle and was able to leave my small village. He used to drink a lot and wasn't such a nice man. It's normal for men to misbehave and you know women have to look the other way." Asking her this question, I could really understand why she gave me this advice. She was a product of what she endured, and that was the best advice she could give me. So here I was getting advice left and right, but I had to pause to see what really made sense for me. I had to stand alone, because that information didn't feel right for me. You need to honor the choices that are right for you, and that means sometimes you are going to have to stand alone. The good news is you're not going to stand alone forever. I tapped into the divine and I was not alone. But you have to be willing to spend time alone to build this connection to your God. I also found a few angels that did understand what I was going through. I was so blessed, especially when the majority of the information coming from the outside seemed so ridiculous and upsetting! There are times when you're feel like you're alone even though in your heart you know it's the right decision. You'll have to learn to be comfortable with standing in that discomfort. Most women run from it because they haven't practiced it. But it's what will keep you moving forward to leave your marriage and make so many other important decisions in your journey.

Creating Effective Boundaries

Remember I was harping about the importance of creating boundaries in an earlier chapter? Well, another big mistake women make when contemplating divorce is they don't know how to create effective boundaries with others. Growing up, I didn't really understand boundaries. My mom would check my mail, snoop in my room, and ask direct and embarrassing questions. Sometimes it felt like being on trial, and I just wanted to duck and hide. An example of this is when my mom asked me about my finances when I was leaving my marriage. This was a very delicate time because my lifestyle would be changing – my husband controlled the finances; he was the breadwinner and I trusted him to do this. I was in a world of tremendous uncertainty about my financial future, and this terrified me.

This question set off an alarm bells in my head. Two reasons being one my husband used money as a means of control and so did my father. I would feel incompetent and inadequate when it came to money. Growing up, my dad would complain if we spent one dollar on something he deemed frivolous. Everything was pretty much frivolous in his eyes. He also came from a family of twelve kids, so I now understand his thinking. He hoarded his money, not spending it when we went out (mom did the spending), and always lived from scarcity mode. If you bought something nice for him, he would hide it away, forget where he put it, and you would never see him using it. We laughed about this because it was just another of his quirks. My mom feared financial instability, so it was really her insecurities placed on me. She always had the fear of not being able to take care of herself, and I absorbed this fear into my adulthood.

I had to start enforcing boundaries with my ex-husband during the divorce because he was also lying to me about our investments and assets. He tried to hide his pension, which was a substantial amount in the beginning of the divorce process. He took a large sum out of our bank accounts without discussing it with me. He also tried to include our mortgage into my alimony check, and meanwhile he was living in the house! The old me would have been scared and paralyzed to do anything. But this time I fought back, stood up for myself, prepared for his moves and protected myself. This experience was setting me up for something greater. The more I used my voice and stood my ground, a stronger person began to emerge. Someone who was becoming financial capable, owning her own voice, and feeling confidence that she was worthy of a better life.

Another example was when my mom asked me how my sex life was. She repeatedly asked me this when my marriage was falling apart. I finally got to a point where I said, "That's none of your business. I'm not going to talk about my marriage with you." Slowly I saw that I was going to have to shut the door on sharing any details with my parents because they were not capable of helping me through this. I became a good student of listening to when prodding questions where afoot so I could start closing the door. I started saying things like, "I'm not going to go there with you; I love and respect you, but we're not opening that door. I'm safe and doing fine, that's all you need to know."

Creating boundaries with your parents brings out your assertiveness, confidence, and helps them to see you in a different way. When you can say "no" to them with compassion and stand your ground, you're demonstrating an inner strength. They will start to respect you or fall away for some time. It's a risk you have to be willing to take in order to step into yourself. What I've noticed is if your parents love you, they will eventually come around. When you challenge them at first, it will feel weird, clunky, and forced when you're doing it. Like riding a bike you will stumble and look silly, but if you stick with it, I promise you it gets easier.

WALKING DOWN ALL THE PATHS

Another key ingredient when you're contemplating divorce is to walk down all the possible paths, scenarios, and outcomes beforehand. If you are going to tell your parents you're thinking about leaving the marriage, then practice this beforehand! You can roleplay with a mentor, trusted friend, or divorce coach to get you prepared. You'll want to use my 1-2-3 process in having this difficult conversation.

Step one: have your answers/decisions planned in advance. Making your decisions beforehand will make you feel more confident and put you at ease.

Step two: be in touch with your inner state – your body and heart.

When you're rattled by something, look inward and feel it instead of reacting outside. If the feeling is too intense, walk away, take a short break, hit the pause button because you have that right. For example, my voice would get shaky when I first started telling my mom, "I don't like when you poke fun at my body," or "Please don't call me selfish." I would use my breath to ground me and put my attention there.

Step three is being aware of the other person's state of mind. Because this will determine if there is an opening for you to share more with them or if it's just not the right time! I realized that my parents weren't ready to hear difficult things about themselves. I had to wait for the right opportunity, and I could sense that because I was attuned to my own body, which allowed me to be more aware of my external environment.

If there's an unwillingness to hear you out time and time again, then that door is not open now. Part of your job is honoring that. It's like someone keeps throwing the ball back in your court, and you throw it back in theirs thinking they will do something different. They will not if they are limited in their ability to do so. They must rise above the clouds of their mind to see clearly. It's also up to the divine spirit to open the door if and when the time is right.

When my dad told me that I was disappointing them when I was leaving my marriage, this set me free. How, you ask? This showed me how much I could really share with my parents. It showed me what they were and were not capable of. This was setting me up to find my own voice and show my leadership communication. I know this sounds horrifying, but I had a choice to make. I could feel like a victim and continue to live by their words, which meant that I would be dying by their words too. Did I really want that for my future self? I'd been living like that all my life, and it was time to do something different. So I chose to learn from this, prepare for more difficult conversations ahead, use it to navigate better. Discernment serves you well when you walk down the paths, because it's like you almost know which path to choose and what is not going to work.

HAVE AN EXIT PLAN!

I learned how important having an exit strategy is if things get too tense and a situation arises. You are not obligated to stay in a space in which you feel threatened; you need to look after your well-being and your mental health first. You can plan, have the 1-2-3 process, and things can still go haywire. That's when you need to safely remove yourself from a situation. An example of this is when my parents argue and fight in front of me, I don't stay there. They had being doing this since childhood, and it was their normal way of communicating. This wasn't normal for me anymore. I've decided ahead of time what to do if that happens in my presence. I tell them to stop, or I leave the room. I don't put myself in that energy anymore. I know some of this stuff may seem radical at first, but you are creating a safe space for yourself and others too. When a room is filled with uplifting and positive energy, it opens the gates for real love and bonding to happen. So the more you can live in and become a role model for that space, magic will happen!

If there's space created for tender moments to happen, a real letting go, then you get to experience the sweetness of life. Growing up, I rarely cried in front of my parents; we didn't show many soft emotions, so this is a process I've had to co-create with them. I had a breakthrough after my divorce. I remember crying to my mom, sharing what I really went through after my divorce. I could do this then because my parents and I were working on our relationship and being more open with feelings. I was telling her how that time was so trying and lonely.

She said, "I'm sorry that happened." It was such a simple moment, but it was filled genuine love. Two people communicating from a heart to heart level. Honestly it's something that I never thought would really happen. But there was a greater force guiding that conversation, plus I was finding resilience and confidence in myself, seeing the good in my parents, all that created space for that moment to happen. I'm falling in love with parents, falling because I've done the work in myself and understand their past. I'm so grateful for tender moments and appreciate the time we have together.

This would not have happened if I was still too afraid to hurt them and stayed in my marriage. This leads me to my final big mistake that women make in contemplating divorce – they don't want to hurt anyone in this process! This sets up a good place to get yourself stuck. Why? Because on one hand, you want freedom, independence, happiness, to feel appreciated and loved. All that is waiting for you when you leave this marriage. On the other hand, you don't want hurt anyone with your needs/desires. Your heart says one thing and your behavior says another. What you're essentially doing is saying other people's needs/wants are more important that mine. And you're actually lying to them and yourself because you truthfully want something different. This is what's really unfair to them because your actions are not coming from a truthful place. If you look closely, you are actually hurting them by not living your honesty. I had a client that, before working with me, she'd tried to leave her marriage for decades! But her husband would get sad, upset, and she couldn't bear to see him like that so she kept staying. I helped her see that she was hurting her husband by living this lie. She was also preventing him and herself from finding real love. Also, developing a life of happiness and authenticity. The divine creator did not create you to hide, play small, and dampen your light. Who is this actually serving? It's not serving you or them.

But…You Don't Want to Hurt Anyone

Another piece to this puzzle is seeing if you can really "hurt" someone. I know your parents may say, "You're hurting me if you do this or that thing." But if you look closely, this is guilt trap made to keep you playing small. They may be sharing some sad stories that they don't want to change and seem to be stuck in. It's not your responsibility to solve this inner hurt for them. They must look at this and work at it the same way you are working on yourself. Yes, your parents can misunderstand you or be upset by your actions, but you don't actually have the ability to hurt them without them giving you their permission. The permission needs to be given in order for that to occur and that experience happens within them the same way it happens in you. Yes, of course there's physical and emotional pain where someone inflicts pain on you. That is not what I'm referring to. Those are very serious situations and should be addressed with caution, urgency, and respect.

YOU'RE NOT RESPONSIBLE FOR OTHER'S HAPPINESS

You are not responsible for making anyone else feel happy. Growing up, my mom would feel low, and it was our job to make her feel better. She had settled into victim mode; when she was treated, given nice things, appreciated by us it was usually short lived because it was coming from the outside. She was trying to solve this deep hurt from the outside and it just wasn't going to happen for her. This brought me sadness when I witnessed it, but I've learned to love my mom from where she is and not try to change her.

This dependency with pleasing my parents set me up for being in marriage where I just kept giving. It was my comfort zone. The one step you can take today is to take stock of how you feel around your parents. Are they draining to be around, do you feel like you've expended a lot of energy with little to show on your end? You can look at your other relationships and you'll began to see patterns. You've set this dynamic up now, and it's time that it's changed. You don't win in dependency because you feel drained because you're feeling an expectation to provide, and it's unfair to them because their happiness should really be on self-start!

HOLIDAY BLUES

Another key thing to develop confidence and resilience to sustain you and your decision to leave the marriage is to pay attention to external forces. What I mean by that is to understand how holidays and planned events can affect your emotional well-being. For example: Valentine's Day. Say you've decided you're leaving your marriage and then Valentine's Day is around the corner. There will be ads on TV, things on social media, friends talking about what they're doing… I want you to be aware of how all that can keep you from moving forward.

Say the 4th of July is around the corner, and that's a huge family holiday. Plan in advance how you would like to handle this. If you're thinking about leaving the marriage, you may want to consider putting some boundaries up so you don't get caught up. For example, say Kali is ready to leave her marriage and knows it in every fiber of her being. Her husband wants to make plans for them to go away and have family time. But she really doesn't feel like doing this. Why? Because it will be planned out to avoid him. She feels like she's giving up time that she'd rather spend on herself. Bottom line, this feels more like an obligation to go away rather than a lovely getaway for her. Kali will see ads for this holiday, her friends will ask her what her plans are, her extended family will want to know what they are doing. If she thinks ahead and sees how these holidays and events will affect her, she can get better prepared for them. This gives her the opportunity to say, "No, I don't want to go away" or "We need to talk" or "I'd like to spend this time alone." Then she'll be affected less by the holidays because she would have seen a way to deal with it before it comes up to bite her in the butt. It's easier to avoid leaving the marriage if you're making vacation plans, celebrating events, and off traveling!

FUEL YOUR INSPIRATION TO LEAVE!

The other part of building confidence and resilience to sustain you in this decision is to find things that feed your inspiration during this process. For me, it was a type of dance called five rhythms, which was a meditative dance. I got to sweat, shake my butt, cry in peace, and release tension. I showed up almost every week, and it was a great way to meet new people. This also helped me dive into music and make playlists to help me release emotions at home. I liked the Cranberries' song "Shattered;" it was like my own life was being shattered, and I had to let go of my old dreams and make way for new dreams. "A New Life" by Jim James is another song that opened up my heartspace and felt my desire for a new life and new possibilities. Music has a way of touching your heartspace, and it allows you to shut out those gremlins and really connect what's important for you. It can uplift you, help you release pain, and take you into your body by dancing!

Another thing that inspired me was to watch transformational movies and read uplifting material! I really gravitated to *Eat, Pray, Love*; *Broken Open*; *A New Earth*; and *Wild*. I always looked for juicy quotes that uplifted my heart and helped me recognize the divine within. I member watching the *Eat, Pray, Love* movie after I read the book, and I just relate to the character's journey of knowing this life wasn't the right fit, doing something different, being scared and having so much guilt, and finally having the courage to let go and be in the unknown. Soften into it. I did go and explore and live in different countries and learn a different language. Be inspired to keep moving; that is the big key here.

THE BUSINESS OF DIVORCE

Another very important part of developing confidence and resilience is to learn about the divorce process. If you're thinking about leaving your marriage, you better understand all avenues legally, financially, your environment, social circles, health-wise, and so forth. See what kinds of divorce options are out there. See what makes sense for you. Get familiar with the business of divorce. What documents do you need to start collecting? Doing this research will put you in the prepare phase and build your confidence. It will also make you feel more confident if you do decide to include your parents in this life decision. Preparing so you know the knowledge before helps you not feel blindsided, and part of you stepping into this new self feeling more independent is taking control of owning knowledge.

I know this sounds scary because you're still preparing to have conversations, but this is part of preparing. You will feel less shaken when you answer questions because you would have done the research for yourself. And you don't have to go it alone. This is a great entry point to elicit a divorce coach. I help clients get ready for tough conversations, to get an overview of the divorce process, and provide access to vetted referral partners. The point is to feel more ready and equipped to move ahead with your decision to leave your marriage.

Some of what I mentioned in this chapter may seem overwhelming and uncomfortable. I just want to leave you with this: know that you're not alone in this process. You have help; you could reach out to divorce coach, reach out to a mentor, you can reach out to your trusted friend who inspires you and believes in you... but the point is that any woman that has been in your position has felt the same things. They're so normal to feel, because you're going through this big life decision that needs to be honored. You can also look at the envisioning work you've done already and see how amazing your life is, what benefits you're receiving, what door is open, and how much you're enjoying life whenever you need a pick-me-up!

Chapter 9

Who's On Your Team? Create the Right Support Circles

EXPOSURE TO DIFFERENT THINKING

Support circles mesh perfectly with the last chapter! "Alone we can do so little; together we can do so much," said Helen Keller. What this really means is that you accomplish so much more when you have the right people by your side. I think of it as my soul tribe – people with whom I share similar values and desires, and who create the space for something magical to happen.

I noticed how women in my culture felt they didn't have support in their marriage. They all got together and complained about the lack of support, and in a way that made them feel supported. But then you have a group complaining and not wanting to solve the issue.

This builds a lot of resentment, fuels arguments, and keeps them stuck. Why? A lot of their energy is going to investing in victim mode, so there's a lot less for them to solve the issue. If you're in this mode, you're often tired, deflated, and unmotivated to go take actions that would uplift and inspire you. You've gotten stuck in a role that you're used to playing very well. The key is to find the right support circles so you're not stuck in this drama. It's so easy to be caught in a web that prevents you from leaving your marriage.

I really needed to rewire my brain, and connecting with supportive role models and social circles is what helped me do that. Meeting new uplifting people helped me stay focus, see things in a different way, and stay open to new possibilities for myself. So, how did I do it? I didn't actually seek out women leadership groups but I found an event at the Omega Institute in Rhinebeck, New York. It was called Women/Men: The Next Conversation, and boy was it enlightening! This event was one of the biggest things that gave me an understanding for difference the between genders. I was able to develop more empathy for males, especially the ones of my culture. I always thought they had it easy because women were doing all the heavy lifting and they were so overbearing.

Tony Porter was a speaker at the conference, and he worked with rehabilitating men in prison that have committed domestic violence crimes against their partner. His work was intriguing because it lifted the veil of why some of these men act/think the way they do. He discovered that these men have repressed emotions since childhood, and they didn't know how to deal with them. They exploded with the full force as adults and had very little understanding of emotional intelligence. Their emotions get shut down at a much earlier age than girls. It's typical for boys to display this conquering energy where they call each other names, put each other down, and make fun of any other boys who act too "feminine." It's like any feminine part was shut down, and they've hardened up, unable to feel their feelings. What I found is with girls, their voice gets shut down later, so they're able to be more in touch with their emotions. Girls are taught to emphasize their prettiness, smartness, and feel it's part of their worth. For example, I saw it was much more acceptable for a boy to be heavy than a girl. It was more acceptable for them to be untidy and have a freeness to wear whatever they choose. We both have masculine and feminine energy within us, so if this is off balance it will keep you trapped. How? You'll be stuck in playing a role and not know your true essence. This is what was happening with both the men and women in my culture. They were falling into play roles and forgetting their true essence. This information helped me step outside my culture and expand my thinking.

MY YOGA TRIBE

I was better informed to see what kinds of people I'd like to connect with. For example, I wanted to find women that uplift each other and build each other up! I wanted to be around women that celebrated their gifts, that could share and open your heart, be vulnerable. Where I could share if I was having a bad day and not feel judged or shamed for it. I was making an emotional leap to find these people. I found some through yoga. I found females that felt good about their body no matter what size, shape, or color. I found women talking about inner strength and emotional well-being. All these things made my heart sing and something inside clicked, saying, "Oh, this are my people!"

In my yoga tribe, we were meeting every week, sharing our roadblocks, what our heart was feeling, and we were all holding the space for each other's story! I remember being assigned to a particular yoga teacher as my mentor. She said, "There's a reason we are meeting, so tell me what's going on?" Then I opened up that I was leaving my marriage and using yoga as a way to help me grow from this. She said, "I was wondering why the universe connected us!" She had just signed the paperwork of her own divorce and got through leaving her culture to create the life she wanted for herself. She said her mom told her, "We women need to bend like the branches of a good tree." She said she was tired of bending! Diving into activities and your passions to meet new and like-minded people will definitely help you stay focused, keep you fueled and help you leave your marriage.

UNIVERSE SENT ME A MOM AND DAD

While my parents couldn't emotionally be there for me in my divorce, the universe brought me a mother figure. My boss was like a mother bear/mentor, and she was a great sounding board. She was a career woman, and she really carved a way for herself. She was very independent, but had a big heart, and there was just something in me that really appreciated that because I had never really grown up around women who had that kind of confidence and independence.

I didn't know it at the time, but she was modeling for me what I wanted for myself. I wanted strength, independence, confidence, and she was exhibiting all of that! She was also a very good friend who I could turn to, go in and share the real highs and lows of leaving my marriage. She genuinely wanted to be there for me, support me, and help me walk towards the path of re-gaining confidence in myself. She held the space without any expectations and judgments. She also challenged me to think higher when I would beat myself up!

Another angel by my side was another old boss of mine. He gave me the opportunity to expand my friendship with a male. I didn't really have much experience with that because of my upbringing. Tony Porter mentioned that men are raised to see women as sexual conquests, objects, and not really as friends. I experienced this in my culture where the boys were separated from the girls so it was hard to form real friendships. It was great to have a role model as a male in this critical time. We hiked, talked about work, and he would guide me and give advice during this time. I remember him saying not to get stuck in silly fights with this divorce. He said to stay focused and continue to let your insight guide you. The universe brought me amazing people in a very difficult time, but I had to trust and get out of my comfort zone. I had to know and trust that these people were out there!

DIVORCED FOLKS AND PROFESSIONALS

Another thing that helped was talking to other divorced folks. I had a friend who was recently divorced, and the woman inspired me. I reached out to her, and we would have dinners together. It was great because here I was, meeting somebody on the other side and they were doing well, dating and finding love. It was inspiring to me that it didn't have to be this ugly demise. It's something dying, but there's something that is being born at the same time. Another option is also thinking about connecting with divorce professionals or divorce groups to learn more about the process. A divorce coach is a great place to start because they can give an overview of the process, they can help walk you through steps and logistics, help you prioritize, and also help you access vetted referral partners and be a sounding board throughout the whole process. I would start putting those antennas up and looking for a trusted person to recruit into your circle as you're changing so you have that support as you move forward. How do you do this? Start by asking for referrals. Then go on their website and see what kind of divorce professional they are. What services do they offer? What kinds of cases do they take? What's their preferred mode of communication? Preparing questions in advance of meeting divorce professionals will be a good use of time and money.

STRANGER DANGER

It can be scary to get out there, especially when you've only known certain social circles and you've been brought up where the gender roles are rigid. I would say you're worth it; you're worth it to step out there and expand your views. Look at different cultures, different types of people and have this hope of meeting people that are where you're moving towards.

Most importantly, when you're meeting new people, stay open. At the same time, use those wonderful instincts that you've been holding in. Listen to your heart, listen to your body, know when a decision is right for you, know who drains your energy and who uplifts you, and notice how you're feeling when you're around someone. I would even use that scale from one to ten; how are you feeling around this person the majority of time? That leads to talking about the difference between cheerleaders and emotional vampires!

So, cheerleaders are people who want to support you and want the best for you. They've got your back and you can start to open up your heart. I'm not talking about people who you're hoping will change, who will see your worth someday, will be convinced to love you and appreciate you in the future. It doesn't work that way. You shouldn't have to convince anyone to be on your side, and you'll be able to spot those types of people the more you learn to have your own back.

I'm talking about relationships where you do not feel judged, and it's almost like a kinship, like yes, I understand you, I've been here, I'll hold your hand and we'll get through this. I don't know, maybe you haven't experienced this, but trust me, it's out there! When you're seeking new people, you're going to do this slowly and with intention. Folks should earn your trust, because not everyone is trustworthy. It's like dipping your toe into the water, you're taking some intel and getting to know this new person. Allow your instincts to guide you, and take stock of what they are sharing with you. This is about co-creating a beautiful relationship where you both are bringing things to the table. Think of it as having a nice picnic outside, and you both need to bring things for it. You get there and each share and enjoy the experience. And you share some more and grow together. It's a process, and remember to be easy with yourself. It takes real guts to step out of your comfort zone and hang with new types of groups. And when you're going in to meet new people through activities, meetings, and events, you want to feel your best, and you want to do your internal work so you can show up with your genuine self and really be there with presence.

DANCING MY HEART TO FREEDOM

I remember going to those five rhythms dancing class. That was one of my first experiences when I was leaving my marriage, and it was it was pretty scary. I had a friend visiting town and she said, "Hey, I do this!" There was a room full of people dancing to music that takes them on a journey. Helping them release pain and really feel uplifted, lighter, brighter. I was on the floor stretching, and I was just thinking, "Please, I don't want any men dancing next to me. That's going to freak me out!" I just felt ugly, so heavy, I had a lot going on inside, and my confidence was definitely shot. But I needed to stay there and do this – I softened into the discomfort. Of course, I just danced in the corner of the room the entire night, but that was a good start!

This went on for months; then I got to the point where I could work the room! I could let loose, look silly, and dance swirls in the middle filled with people. This really helped me regain my confidence. But things need to be clunky and uncomfortable first. I needed to question things and go through that ugly duckling phase. I saw that not feeling your best is the human struggle, and when we can look at each other in the eyes, share, and open up, that's where the magic happens. I will say I was a five rhythms dancing queen, because I enjoyed going to it and stuck it out and was doing it for years. I just could go anywhere in that room and had a real blossoming because I got out of my comfort zone.

The thing about connecting with supportive role models and social circles is that you will start to release people who no longer like the new you. They will start to fall out of your life, and it can be sad at first. I remember losing two dear friends because I'd outgrown our relationship. When you meet people on the same plane as you, you're just ready to go off and seek greener pastures together! You feel a sense of aliveness and freedom that was missing before. There's also a kinship and a flow. On the flip side, when you're changing, you can surely inspire change in your existing circle, and that's what happened with my parents. I'm so grateful for that; I'm over the moon, because I truly I did not expect that. I think I created the space for them to be more who they are and for me to be more who I am, and the divine came in.

Meeting new folks and allowing new social circles into your life is supposed to feel scary and wonky. It's just part of the process, and if you can, think back to when you learn to do something new. How awkward that was, scary, how you had moments where you looked silly, you felt like you were going to fall flat on your face. That's the same thing here. Here's an exercise – think about the traits you used to overcome that challenge. Now, list them out and see what you can use to benefit you in this transition! You have to apply them here, have patience, discipline, and a whole lot of humbleness with yourself. Chuck Yeager was the first American test pilot who broke through the sound barrier. When they interviewed him, he commented that just before he was breaking through the sound barrier, his cockpit shook like crazy. It's the same thing here! You're going to be shaking because you're doing something out of your comfort zone. So, buckle up, and try your best to enjoy the ride!

Chapter 10

Taking the Leap and Divine Communication

PEOPLE CAN ONLY GIVE YOU WHAT THEY HAVE TO GIVE

Now that you've gotten some tips on knowing what the right support is and how to find it, let's dive into "taking the leap." Yes, this is what you've been preparing for. It's time to blast off with all the knowledge and skills you've acquired along this journey. You can do this! You got this! I know you're unsure and maybe a little nervous, but that's what happens when you are facing a fear. Have you heard the saying about fear means false evidence appearing real? Well, that is what fear turns out to be. It just means you haven't done this before, it rattles you, and the best way to move forward is to look it in the face. Once you have this experience under your belt, I promise you it will get easier, and you will be adding another accomplishment to your wonderful tool belt. But most of all, you owe it to yourself to reach your own potential. There are gifts in you waiting to be unlocked and experienced!

Here you get to own your voice with others and demonstrate this new you. But first, let's understand that people can only give you what they have to give. This means if you go to an apple tree expecting to get oranges, then you're going to be very disappointed. If your parents are unable to give their blessing and support in this decision, it's because they aren't capable of it. That's why we did all that work with understanding your parents' past and your parental relationship. Realizing this and accepting it was so freeing for me with my own parents. I let go of my need to want them to be different. Instead, I appreciate them for their gifts, quirks, and eccentricities, which really allows me to enjoy our moments much more. Letting go of my attachment is what created the space for us to deepen our bonds.

Your parents probably have certain expectations of you; it's their practice to release that in their own time. The quicker you release your expectation for them to be a different way, the quicker you'll move through this process. You should be more aware of what you'd be walking into if you do decide to share with them your decision to leave this marriage. If you know that they will have a meltdown and it would be unproductive and hinder your progress, then that needs to be honored. Of course, the decision is entirely up to you, and you should have a sense now as to whether it makes sense for you, or if this is not a good idea at this time. This can mean you've arrived at leaving your marriage on your own, regardless of your parents desires for you. You can choose to tell them, not tell them, or even tell them later on. Just tap into your heartspace and uncover that right next decision. You've also probably worked out all the outcomes and scenarios, so this will also better inform you of what to do.

KNOWING WHERE TO PUT YOUR TRUST

Next, let's focus on knowing where to put your trust. Pastor T.D. Jakes says, "Don't tell your big dreams to small minded people." I love this because it helped me see that I don't need to share everything with everyone, especially my parents if they're incapable of processing it. This would just lead to worries and stress, and you surely won't get help planning for this dream. In fact, the opposite will happen, and you will be hampered down by this negative energy. Instead, find people who will provide shade from the sun, shelter you from the rain, inspire you with their magnificence, and will champion your wins. When you focus on knowing where to put your trust, you will start to confide in the right people. It will feel like a whole world of support opens up to you. Why? Because you are sharing with individuals that are nonjudgmental, not reactive when you share heavy news, show empathy, have good listening skills, and are a good sounding board.

This will light something up inside you, where you'll feel some of the weight come off and more clearly see your next step. Once you experience compassion on this level, it will be hard to want anything less.

REST, TAKE BREAKS, GET OUT OF THERE!

Taking the leap requires a lot of energy because you are transforming, so have rest breaks, patience, and an exit strategy; these will serve you very well. If you remember back to when you were studying for a test, you had to carve out energy for that. You probably had to develop a laser focus, say no to things in order to meet your goals, and rest so you felt recharged to keep going! This is no different. This is a major life decision, so putting in more focus and effort will help you get through the process. Rest breaks can mean anything from getting enough sleep at night to taking a break from a difficult conversation. For example, if you are telling your parents you are contemplating divorce, this may need to be discussed several times before it makes sense to them. This can mean giving you and them time to process and let the conversation unfold and sink in. You have every right to stop the conversation if you are feeling drained or if things get heated. Go get some air, get a cup of tea, do some breathing exercises, or go for a run and return to this when you feel recharged. Most women make the mistake of staying in the conversation too long, where it becomes too heavy and unproductive. This can lead to reactive behavior and impulsive decision-making. You want to have an exit strategy if things get really ugly and out of control. For example, if your parents are calling you names, yelling, or playing the victim card and your intuition says, "It's time to get out of here," you have to stay present, so you listen to your wonderful intuition and do not fall prey to your parents' hooks.

RELEASE YOUR ATTACHMENT TO THE OUTCOME

Another important point to taking the leap is to release any attachment to the outcomes. It's not your job to convince, seek approval, or try to coax anyone into agreeing with your choices. If something sits right with you, then that is good enough. Being okay with sticking with your decisions, even though the outcomes may not support it, also needs to be honored. Women get too caught up in wanting to do things right, in wanting everything to work out just perfectly. But sometimes life throws us lemons and we really need to make that darn lemonade! It's a great gift to yourself to practice the art of surrendering. This is when you give the space for the higher source to guide you and the matter at hand. This is not easy, and it's like working a muscle at the gym, you will need to put in the practice. Releasing your attachment to the outcome also frees up so much more energy for you to go forward with your decision to leave the marriage. You're not stuck in wanting things to be different anymore. There are a lot of factors to consider when you're contemplating divorce, so any extra energy you have will serve you well!

YOUR BODY NEEDS TO CATCH UP!

Another part of the leap process is to give your body time to catch up to the "New You." What do I mean? You are literally rewiring your brain to think, feel, and act a new way. Your body will have to go through its own process to support you in your new way of making decisions. It's like when you take dance class, and you're learning the new steps. You can feel rigid, off balance, flighty, and unsure if this is going to work out. Know there are different stages to learning, so you have to develop patience with yourself in this process. You are essentially stepping into a new role, a role where you say no more often, you challenge others more, you have opinions that are openly expressed, and you stand up for yourself. This will feel foreign to your body, so take it easy and be patient with yourself. That new woman you are envisioning who's reaping the benefits of leaving her marriage has big shoes to fill, so you need structure, discipline, commitment, and trust that you'll get there! That's why feeling into your body is so important. I talked about this in a previous chapter. Diving into a new passion or learning a new skill helps you with this rewiring process and gets you out of your comfort zone!

TRUST LIFE TO GUIDE YOU

Look for signs and signals, and trust life to keep guiding. You've made it this far, and you keep showing up! Good job! You're so close to crossing a big threshold for yourself. The way you stay on track to leave your marriage is to look for the signs and signals, and believe that life is taking you where you need to go. We talked about how your intention for leaving the marriage can be linked to a bigger purpose for yourself. You don't know what amazing things are in store for you. I've worked with clients who've gone on to climb mountains in Peru, complete their dissertation in their fifties, fall in love with their body through salsa classes, find a real love partnership, and even gone on to starting a new business. Life is filled with endless possibilities and staying awake to its communication to you is imperative. When you do this, you're looking for things that seem like nudges or coincidences, or seem familiar. Maybe you were feeling like its time to share the news with your mom and all of a sudden you get a call from her right after! Or you've been feeling super exhausted, and then you get a glowing recommendation from your best friend about a spa she just tried. Another example is if you get up in the morning with a feeling that you need to go to the farmers market today. It doesn't make sense because your kitchen is fully stocked, but you decide to go anyway and you end up meeting an old childhood friend. The universe is always talking, you just have to be alert.

I remember when I decided to move out of New York and travel to Costa Rica and Peru after my own divorce. I always seem to be taken care of by the universe. Here I was, traveling alone, and this was going to be my first big trip by myself. I was scared and I didn't know what I'd encounter, but my intuition was guiding me along the way. For example, I was supposed to take a bus from San Jose to Puerto Viejo. I didn't speak Spanish, and the taxi took me from my hotel back to the airport. I was supposed to be dropped off at an area so I could get this bus. We left the airport to go to find this bus stop and there in my view was an American food chain. I remember the tour operator said they were located in the parking lot of this chain. Now, I don't know if this was the right one but my intuition said to go there and I followed it. Sure enough, it was that location, and I made my bus on time!

Another sign was my first day walking on the beach scared and hoping I won't get robbed. It was pretty desolate, but so beautiful. I was feeling a little frightened, then out comes a friendly lab from a brush path to greet me! Along with it were a husband and wife, and the husband's shirt said New York. All of this comforted me because it seemed so familiar. Another sign was when I met a young woman who had just gone through a bad break up. Turns out, we had similar experiences and childhood stories! She was on a soul journey too, and it's like I was meeting a younger version of myself. I had asked the universe to send me some friends on this journey and met her the very next day in yoga. Another sign was when I felt ready to leave Costa Rica, but had not planned my next stop. In fact, I thought I'd stay there the whole time and return to New York. But I felt this restlessness inside, alerting me that it was time to leave. I was feeling pressure to know my next step and then just let that go. When I did, I met people who were sharing an amazing time they experienced in Peru. There my next stop was born, because I just paused to listen.

One of my most life-defining communications from the universe was my time in Machu Picchu. There, I climbed up on the sun gate and I was standing above a mountain top. I could even see the base with its snaking river and clouds hugging the mountain ridge. The mountain was covered with luscious green plants, and it looked so ominous. I remember taking in the view and getting lost in the spellbinding raw beauty. Then the words, "I will never forsake you, I will never forsake you, I will never forsake you," vibrating through my body and heart. It was like waves of love gently bathing me. It was so overwhelming that I started crying and breathing ever so slowly. I felt this ethereal bubble of love engulfing me for a while, and it was like time stopped. Just before that, I'd seen a hummingbird and, according to the Inca tradition, it's a blessing to see a hummingbird in Machu Picchu. It means you are guided, loved, and looked after. It means your dreams will come true and you just have to stay conscious to life. Ever since then, hummingbirds have been with me in my journey. I have the pleasure of seeing them every day in Portland. I feel they are auspicious and they provide signs that blessings will be arriving soon. They also reminded me how blessed I already am. To experience a force greater than myself guiding me is so humbling, and it makes me walk in light every day. I wish that for you too in this journey.

Chapter 11

A Broken Map – Not Knowing How to Navigate Changing Tides

BEING UNCLEAR OF HOW TO NAVIGATE

A lot of the problems happen when you face obstacles and are unsure of how to navigate them. This sets up the perfect recipe to getting stuck and not being able to leave your marriage. In this chapter, I'll cover the hooks that get you, making you feel stuck, confused, overwhelmed, and prevent you from leaving your marriage. First, I'll show you how confusion is a big culprit in this game. If you don't know where you are going, then you won't get there. Being unclear and unsure of the right next step for you is one of the biggest obstacles that keep women feeling stuck. All of sudden, you're are thinking about all the surmounting obstacles you need to face, and these thoughts cripple you from even trying. This makes you look backward and not forward, so you get stuck. Then, because you can't see through the tunnel, you can't really decipher what feels right for you. It's like you're moving through this major decision with foggy brain, and this will knock out any confidence you have in yourself to do this.

NOT UNDERSTANDING YOUR PARENTAL RELATIONSHIP

Another obstacle is not understanding your parental relationship. This is so key in order to navigate inter-actions, communication, and knowing what is right to share with them. Understanding your parents gives you insight into why they think the way they do, where their hangs ups and critical behavior came from, and it prepares you for their reactions ahead of time. When you see their behavior ahead of time, then you are less "hooked" by it. For example, my mom loves to complain about her relationship with my dad. She says how he doesn't appreciate her cooking. She wishes he would tell her how she did a good job, the food tastes so good, and it's like she's reciting a monologue when she shares this. I've been hearing this since my childhood, so to me I've learned to accept this story of hers. Not that I'm not saying that my father can't be a little more appreciative, what I'm saying is that this used to hook me. I used to try my best to cheer her up, make her feel she is loved, until I realized that this was a bottomless pit of need for reassurance and love. So, if you find yourself buying into your parents' victim stories, it will surely hook you. Also you're not able to flip the switch and change the conversation if you don't see what is really going on.

Another factor is you won't develop the empathy and understanding for your parents journey. This is so critical because it goes back to that Gandhi quote, "Be the change you wish to see." Once you have love for your parents' journey, then it's easier to be a light for them and inspire change. But until then, this serves as a major obstacle because you're still stuck with that child-parent dynamic where you're looking for approval, pleasing them, and not really understanding your own power. I also want to add there's a heavy energy/dense energy that can exist. If you ever see your parents suffering, it viscerally feels like a part of you is in chaos. For example when my mom screams/yells at my dad and I'm in the room – I can feel it shaking my own cells. I can feel this toxic energy moving in me. It's almost like breathing in car fumes in a closed garage! It can creep into your thinking, feeling, and affect the way you operate. This is not good for anyone! Some find a way to numb this by becoming hardened/less sensitive to yelling. I find when you armor up your pain, then you can't listen to your heart. You can't live from a true place because you're no longer soft to life, so you can't hear the signs it's giving you.

UNCLEAR OF YOUR REAL INTENTION FOR LEAVING YOUR MARRIAGE

Another obstacle is not uncovering your real intention for leaving the marriage. The real reason needs to be uncovered so it sustains you in your decision. Until then, you'll be flopping around like a fish out of water, unsure of what direction is right for you because your gremlins will be working over time! And if you don't know what direction is right for you, then you'll be making decisions that don't serve your higher goal to leave this marriage. Uncovering your real intention also helps you stay motivated and grounded in the process.

UNSURE OF WHAT DECISION IS RIGHT OR WRONG FOR YOU

When you're unsure of your decisions, it will cause you to run around in circles, and you waste precious time and years. Your decisions will be wishy washy, and you'll be causing yourself and others more confusion. Whatever decision you make, you won't be able to stick to it, because you'll always be questioning yourself. Contemplating divorce is already filled with so much uncertainty, so this just fuels the flame. For example, say Nira desperately wants to leave her marriage. She's been hinting indirectly to her husband that she's unhappy in the marriage. She works up the courage to tell him how unhappy she is, and he gets upset. He gets angry, calling her ungrateful, that she doesn't appreciate him and she should be so lucky for all he's done, like putting her through school, being her mom's therapist, and raising their children. When this happens, she leaves the room and pretends she never voiced these concerns. They've been doing this for decades. She keeps making the decision to avoid it and pretend everything is fine between them. She's unsure of really what decision is right for her. So, she keeps doing the same thing over and over again. This costs her years of being unhappy, and makes her really confused as to how to fix this problem. If you make a decision not right with your heart, you'll also suffer the consequences of it by feeling this restlessness within. It's like your heart is trying to push you to listen, but you're not downloading the message. This creates more suffering and hopelessness.

YOU HAVEN'T ENVISIONED LEAVING THE MARRIAGE

Yet another obstacle that leaves you feeling trapped is that you haven't envisioned leaving the marriage. If you can't see it, then you can't create it into the material plane for yourself. A lot of performers, athletes, artists talk about how creating it in their mind, body, and soul first is what gave them a great outcome. Amy Purdy, the 2014 Sochi Paralympic bronze medalist lost her legs early on in her life due to Meningococcal Meningitis. She talks about her climb back to herself on Oprah's *Super Soul Sunday*. Amy says that she could feel herself on that mountain, she could feel the wind, and see she was there. She envisioned being able to snowboard again and has inspired millions of people. Furthermore, scientists are now finding that our inner feelings, emotions, and thoughts are linked to being able to create the kind of life we want for ourselves. For example, in the TV series *Missing Links* by Gregg Braden, they conducted an experiment where scientists found that emotions affect our DNA. Envisioning leaving your marriage also gives you the opportunity to see how your new life could look. If you're not spending the time to do that and only focusing on your current reality, then you'll feel like you're just getting by the day. Your energy is not going towards the right things to help you leave this marriage. For example, if Jane spends most of her time complaining and feeling powerless in her marriage, it leaves less energy for her to think of another possibility. She may have buried passions in her heart like studying pottery or living in a different country. But if she can't tap into that space emotionally and physically, then she is doomed to stay in her current reality.

YOUR LACK OF CONFIDENCE AND RESILIENCE

Another obstacle that gets women stuck is lack of confidence and resilience to sustain them in this journey. If you're not building your confidence by working on yourself, then you'll be knocked down and stay down pretty quickly. I'm sure there's been times where you wanted to leave this marriage before and you just kept giving up on the idea because you kept getting side tracked with more "important things." It's so easy to talk yourself out of something if your confidence is super low! Let's look at Sarah, who hasn't learned to speak up for herself in her marriage. Her husband harps on her capabilities and calls her stupid pretty often. She doesn't ever know what it feels like to do a single thing right in his presence. She feels like a failure and is always anxious around him. If she's trapped in feeling unworthy, shaking in her voice, and depressed, it will be hard to build confidence and move forward to changing her life. It takes discipline, focus, roleplaying, assessing scenarios and outcomes beforehand, taking rest, rejuvenation, and much more to get to the point where you have a readiness to leave your marriage. This takes so much dedication because you really have to change the way you've been operating. This can mean helping out your parents less and less, doing less at home, saying no more, and women get stuck because they don't have the resilience built into their process.

UNAWARE OF THE FIVE BIGGEST MISTAKES WOMEN MAKE

Another hook that prevents you from leaving your marriage is not being aware of the five biggest mistakes that keep you stuck. If you're not practicing being alone, standing alone, letting go of headtrash, creating boundaries, and releasing the idea of not wanting to hurt others – these pitfalls will keep you locked in a cycle. This cycle is playing small and not stepping into your own light. I like the Einstein quote, "The definition of insanity is doing the same thing over and over and expecting different results."

Let's consider Mary, who wants to leave her marriage but doesn't want to hurt her husband. She wants him to get on the same page so they can then get a divorce. But what if he is not capable of providing you his blessing to leave the marriage? She's making the mistake of not wanting to hurt him, so she continues to stay in the marriage.

NOT HAVING THE RIGHT SUPPORT CIRCLES

Not having the right support circles to leave the marriage is another issue that can hang you up. Have you heard the phrase that you are the average of the five people you spend the most time with? If you've been around people who weigh you down, break you down, think less of you, break you down to build themselves up, this will not equal forward momentum for you. It's critical for you to get outside your comfort zone and seek new people, new thinking, experiences that uplift and inspire you to be a better version of yourself. One of the major reasons women don't leave their marriage is because their closest friends/loved ones give them poor advice. They essentially minimize or devalue your needs/wants. Suppose Jade wants to leave her marriage and she keeps being told that her life is perfect. She has a good provider and her kids go to the best schools. She doesn't have to cook or clean and can buy nice things for herself. Her friend also says, you don't have it as bad as these other women. I would stick this out. If Jade continues to keep this kind of company, her chances for seeing new possibilities and making different choices will not happen. The wrong support circles make you feel like you're asking for too much, you're being a dreamer, or what you want doesn't exist for women like you. I would be vigilant with whom you spend your time with, because that is very telling about which direction you'll go.

DON'T WANT TO LEAP

I like this quote by Anais Nin: "And the day came when the risk to remain tight in a bud was more painful than the risk it took to bloom." There comes a time when you have to leap, but if you don't, then you're doomed to stay the way you are in the situation you're in. You're unable to take the leap, and it's like a failure-to-launch thing happening. You're super afraid of what the future can hold for you. This obstacle is tied to the others because you haven't done the necessary work to leap! You haven't learned to own your own voice with others and release your attachment to any outcomes. You lack conviction in your words, and this will not get you very far in your ability to move forward. You'll still feel dependent on what your parents think and how they treat you. You'll continue seeking their approval and feeling really upset when they're not listening to you or taking you seriously.

You'll continue to feel frustrated in your marriage, even scared to talk to your parents, frightened to stand up for yourself, and you won't be able to leave your marriage. I've seen time and time again how adults turn back into children when they have to face their parents. It's like time freezes and they're back to talking in their little girl voice to appease their parents. Their parent could be demanding that they tell them what time they will be back home? Why are they wasting their money on that? Why are they eating junk food? It's like they've stepped outside of their own body and don't have command of the situation. This is the classic case of being stuck in winning your parents' hearts at the cost of your own. You haven't mastered the art of owning your own voice and standing in your own truth, so leaving this marriage will be so much more daunting to you.

Chapter 12

Leaving or Staying in the Marriage and My Wishes for You!

I wrote this book to connect to your dying soul, to find you so you would wake up and pay attention to that fire inside. It's trying to tell you something so very important, and guess what? Your life depends on your ability to listen to it. I wrote it to connect with you to help you see there is another way in life a way to freedom, choice, and okay with just being. It's okay to be alone, to test the waters. Miraculous things happen when you do. I wrote this book because I know you're frightened of being alone, it's a deep fear that you learned young, and it holds you hostage. Until you really look at where that fear came from, it will keep you trapped. That's what this book wants of you. I want you to dig through the rubble and connect your own dots to see it's not so bad as you think. Like nature shows us with its brilliant colors, majestic power, rejuvenating qualities, and sheer resilience, you, too, possess what it takes to transform!

THE IMPORTANCE OF GOING

I hope you've enjoyed this road map to preparing you to leave your marriage. By now, you see that you need to see clearly first before you can really take any meaningful steps. I hope my personal story gave you hope and insight into how this can be done, and it can be done with the divine by your side. My steps are easy to understand, and it takes a level of bravery to follow them. You will stumble, you will be confused at times, but you have everything you need to get you through the process. You can clear the confusion with the tools given to access your heart, body, and that which is really true for you. Also, the understanding of your parents' past and how that affects you is so vital in overcoming this challenge and making peace to step into this new stage of your life. The stage is accepting yourself more and taking action that supports it even if it ruffles a few feathers. When we can understand the shoes our parents have walked in, a rush of compassion enters and guides us to soften in this process.

Getting intentional is what keeps you grounded and allows your heart to soar. In this journey, you have to uncover your why because it's what sustains you. Your why for leaving this marriage will lead you to other great moments in your life. You will get to the point where you'll know when something is right for you, and you'll get to the business of doing it quicker and quicker! Our intention for doing things also births confidence because our action is propelled by the why. It's as if the action is being done to you, and you are a mere bystander. Okay, maybe it's more like a co-creating, where you are inserting yourself with source so they elevate the process instead of derailing it with your ego.

Once you've gotten your intention for leaving the marriage, it's so ever important to envision your outcome. Seeing this beforehand lights you up, it feeds your heart, and gives you motivation to leave. Why? Because you've seen it in your mind, and felt it in your heart and body. You've already lived the experience, so you see what's possible for yourself. When external forces come to derail you it will pale in comparison to this great vision you've created. Envisioning is the key to stepping into this new chapter of you.

Like all good athletes know, preparation is key to having a successfully outcome. When you know you've honed your body, heart, and mind, you can show up to the challenge fully without attachment to the outcome. When you've walked down all the scenarios and seen all the possible outcomes you feel well equipped for what's ahead. Even if it comes in the form of torrential downpours and massive flooding. Why? Because you know how to refuel, rest up, and you've got an exit strategy in place! You know the pitfalls, and you know your own hooks, so this may even be a little enjoyable.

You don't have to do this alone. You're doing the work to find your "team you." It's the right support circle that will be your cheerleaders and you can confide in with peace in your heart. You can show your full self and not feel judge or reprimanded. You can share and release some of that weight you're carrying. Your circle will help you see the light at the end of the tunnel and keep you focused. These individuals will be helping you discover this "new you." How? As you learn to trust and confide in those who are "for" you, it will allow other expressions to burst up and out of you. You will become more and more recognizable to your own self. That is, your light will be beaming more bright. Your support circles will also have knowledge to help you leave your marriage. From a divorce coach to a gifted lawyer, you will begin to feel like you can move through this.

You'll move towards a readiness to jump with abandonment, but know that you have a parachute of tools to help you along the way. You'll see more and more whom you can trust and who is not trust-worthy. You'll look for patterns in conversations to quickly see *are these people my cheerleaders or not?* You'll build a closer bond with your body because it's going to be sending a whole lot of signs and signals your way. The key difference is you'll be listening to them now. You'll be kinder and more patient with yourself because you see that's the key to good decision making and moving this process along. Most of all, you'll feel that divine power guiding your steps, you'll be walking into rooms with that power by your side. You'll be celebrating that connection to it because you know you've come back home to yourself.

You'll see more obstacles ahead of time and know how to maneuver before it has a chance to shake you. Knowing the obstacle is the first step to defeating it. You'll also see when you need help and can't do this alone. That is a great thing to know, because you'll be acknowledging when it's time to seek the right resources. This will help you make better decisions when you are getting ready to leave the marriage.

WHAT'S YOUR LIFE WORTH TO YOU?

I wrote this book because my heart was dying when I went through this for myself. You are at a critical point where your heart is asking you to listen to it. It may even need to resuscitate because you've lost so much of yourself in this marriage. You will keep hiding it, pretending, and only you will continue to carry this burden. The volcano bubbling inside will become uncontrollable, and you'll have to find grander ways to suppress it. How long are you willing to continue to smile, look pretty, cater to everyone's needs, all while it's killing you inside? Stop racing, slow down, stop agreeing to play this part when you really want to be doing something else. Do you think of yourself as a liar? Probably not, but when you pretend everything is okay you're lying to both yourself and others. In fact keeping up this facade makes you a liar. You're better than that! Listen to your heart. Your heart wants to pull you in another direction. I know it's scary, I've been there, but what life do you have if the meaning is being sucked out? Pay attention to your soul, connect to that future women you envisioned for yourself. Your life will be filled with a lot less colors, more anxiousness, and unhappiness. Is it worth it to continue feeling this dreaded loneliness? This confusion? This unworthiness? This stripping away of yourself?

THE LIGHT WAITING FOR YOU

It's so important for you to leave this marriage because your soul will feel free. You have important work to do in this world and if you are living a lie everyday, it will not serve that work. You have new people to meet, new experiences to have, and lots more growing to do. This will inspire your parents and any loved ones because they will be seeing a transformation right before their eyes. You will become a role model for the women in your culture, and this is your way of breaking the cycle for the younger generation. They need to see how living your truth can be done, and the positive example you give them will be so inspiring. If you choose to not leave the marriage, then you close the door to lots of other things. Things like your own health and well-being. Your ability to have ease and laughter and lightness in your daily life. It's like you'll be carrying around a backpack of "junk" on your back. You'll be taking that everywhere you go, and it will become heavier and heavier. I remember when it was time for me to leave New York. The longer I stayed there, the more it felt like walking through molasses. The things I used to enjoy all of sudden became so heavy to endure. That's when you know it's time to leave and to honor this feeling.

You also will be continuing to lie to love ones and not allowing them to learn about themselves. For example, your husband probably has some lessons to learn and can't do it in this marriage. He needs to feels what it's like for things to not go his way. Give him the chance to develop his own self-growth by facing his own issues. Another example is not changing the dynamic with your parents. They will still see you as a child that needs to be rescued, looked after, and is a bit fragile. They would not see the empowered and assured you. They'll miss all this wonderful potential buzzing inside of you. Shouldn't they witness this before they leave this earth? It may help them see some things differently about themselves. I know when I left my marriage on my own terms, I gained my parents' respect. My mom has become more empowered in her relationship and stands up to my dad's bad habits a little more.

You have the ability to dive into new experiences like exploring a place you've always wanted. Maybe learning a new language or joining a painting class. Whatever adventure is waiting you'll have more headspace, energy, and time to do it. Because you've broken the chains you've placed on yourself. You've left this marriage and are enjoying what your heart really wants. You're growing in your independence and freedom. You are making choices for you and don't have that heaviness of having to look after someone when your heart is not there. You'll stop that wishy-washy behavior, and know when you go to events or meet people, you're there because you really want to be and not because you feel obligated to. You'll stop betraying yourself by putting everyone else's needs in front of your own. You'll also learn how to come to the party feeling your best because you've rested, and been nice to yourself!

MY HEART WILL BE SAD FOR YOU

I feel sad if you don't discover your potential. Leaving this marriage is calling you to be a better version of yourself. It hurts me if you're still stuck in a marriage where you feel unloved and unappreciated. It saddens me to think you are serving the needs of your parents and feeling like it's taking a toll on you. I know because I've been there. When your well is almost empty, and you keep giving and giving, it feels like a prison. It feels lonely and you're riddle with anxiousness. You questioning yourself and doubting your worthiness is painful for me to think about. Why? Because I know that suffering so dearly. It's like feeling like a shell of a woman where you drift from one thing to the next thing with hopelessness. You keep grasping on the outside for things to fill you up, but nothing is working. Eventually you reach a breaking point.

This is vital for you to know because our greatest moment of suffering is also a loud thud over the head. It's our heart saying, "No, silly, I keep directing you this way, will you stop and *listen to me!*"

My wish for you is to cut through the noise in your head. Things like…

- I'm not good enough
- I don't matter
- I'm not important
- My voice is not important
- Who am I to want that?
- I can't say "no"
- Everyone depends on me
- I'm not doing a good enough job
- I'm not contributing enough
- My wish for you is to do the following:
- Balance your needs with the needs of others, and that includes your parents!

- Feel confident to own your own voice with others no matter the situation (friend circles, work colleagues, family, associations, relationships, etc.)

- I want you to stay true to yourself and free yourself from playing roles

- I want to you to set healthy communication boundaries for yourself and with others.

- I want you to put yourself first when problem solving so you get clarity right away about your own wants/intentions/values/desires. So often you think about others needs that it distorts your own reality!

- I want you to carve out time for these five things self-reflection, self-awareness, self- respect, self-acceptance, and self-love!

- I want you to have the courage to leave a bad marriage/relationship. With this book, I elevate the divorce process, giving you a new set of eyes… helping you to see a way filled with opportunities!

- I want you to break a cycle of "waiting" for love, for your partner to "come to their senses," to make decisions for you…waiting in the wings for someone, I want you to take back control of your own life!

- I want you to say yes to things/people from a *real* place. A place that's firmly rooted in knowing who you really are and what you really stand for! When you say yes from your heartspace, you'll show up more fully alive, and this affects your presence and ripples out in your surroundings.

- I want you to be brave – to try new things, discover your talents, gifts, and take risks, make space to bring out your own uniqueness.
- I want you to get comfortable with the discomfort that transformation brings!
- Much love, light, and blessings to you!

Acknowledgements

I'd love to give thanks to the Author Incubator team for making this dream a reality. I especially want to thank Dr Angela, Mehrina, Moriah, and Aicha for working with me so closely to bring forth this book. There was so much packed away in my head and the Author Incubator team gave me a way to translate it on the page. I now get a chance to impart the knowledge I learned to other women in a way that will make a difference. I believe these women were not being served, and my hope is to bring some light in what can be such a dark time in their lives. I also get to live my dream of helping women in a bigger way because they can have access to this material from all over the world.

I want to thank Sharon Blondina, one of my angels. Without her, this book would not have even been a possibility. She was one of the first women to have my back during my own divorce. She taught me what a strong woman looks like and reminded me of my value. She was a guide for me in what was such a difficult time. My heart will be forever grateful to you!

A big thank you to Sham and Susan who were wonderful sounding boards, and helped me navigate this process. You both helped me feel more and more confident to leave my miserable marriage. You also guided me towards my confidence and standing up for myself. It meant a lot to have you two by my side in this very confusing time!

I want to thank Denise Hedges who helped me make some more of my biggest leaps in my life. Leaps like living abroad in other countries on my own and not knowing anyone there. She also helped me start my own new chapter in Oregon by helping me craft a plan to move from east to west coast. Again she encouraged me to go towards what was placed in my heart. She too was a good role model, strong, and independent thinker. She also had a kind way of communicating that helped move me further in the coaching process! She's helped me clear a lot of my gremlins and challenged me in a way that got me out of my comfort zone. Denise also has helped start me towards doing envisioning work to create the life I want for myself. Some of the tools I teach in this book unfolded by working with Denise. She is my good friend, and I'm so appreciative for having her in my life.

I want to thank Divorce Coaching Inc. created by Pegotty and Randy Cooper. Their Certified Divorce Coach program was a great start to getting out there and practicing this work. I've learned a lot from the CDC program, and my clients get to benefit from the knowledge they've gathered! Pegotty, thank you for your soft but direct way of teaching. You always seem to know what to say and I had so many light bulb moments with your teaching. I also love the sound of your voice!

I want to thank myself. It's been a journey to get to this point of in my life and also to create a piece of work that will help set women free from heavy circumstances. I've worked so hard to arrive here. I've had to change my way of thinking, release self doubt, befriend a lot of uncertainty, and get out of my comfort zone in big ways. Here's a pat on the back to me for making these gigantic leaps

Thank You

Thank you! I've enjoyed sharing this journey with you. I want you know this is just the beginning of great things for yourself. Continue to show up and do the work. Learn to trust and continue to touch into that space of something bigger guiding you.

As a thank you, I've created a video series if you're thinking about leaving your marriage that will give you tons of information on how to navigate this process. Each morning for seven days, you'll receive a video sharing my secrets to leaving your marriage. Sign up at www.stillnessblooms.com

You're here to do amazing things, and I'd to be a resource along the way! I'll be drinking my favorite tea, so grab your yummy beverage and let's spend some quality time together!

About the Author

Peeling away the veils of cultural taboos, CINDY GUNRAJ bravely left a stifling marriage and deepened bonds with her parents. She's a certified divorce coach who helps women contemplating divorce who need their traditional parents' blessing to leave the marriage. She's also a professional speaker and has spoken at United Nations, Unicef, and Dress for Success. Cindy loves hiking, meditation, and lives in Portland, Oregon with her corgi, Joy, and partner David.

DIFFERENCE
P R E S S

About Difference Press

Difference Press is the exclusive publishing arm of The Author Incubator, an educational company for entrepreneurs – including life coaches, healers, consultants, and community leaders – looking for a comprehensive solution to get their books written, published, and promoted. Its founder, Dr. Angela Lauria, has been bringing to life the literary ventures of hundreds of authors-in-transformation since 1994.

A boutique-style self-publishing service for clients of The Author Incubator, Difference Press boasts a fair and easy-to-understand profit structure, low-priced author copies, and author-friendly contract terms. Most importantly, all of our #incubatedauthors maintain ownership of their copyright at all times.

LET'S START A MOVEMENT WITH YOUR MESSAGE

In a market where hundreds of thousands of books are published every year and are never heard from again, The Author Incubator is different. Not only do all Difference Press books reach Amazon bestseller status, but all of our authors are actively changing lives and making a difference.

Since launching in 2013, we've served over 500 authors who came to us with an idea for a book and were able to write it and get it self-published in less than 6 months. In addition, more than 100 of those books were picked up by traditional publishers and are now available in book stores. We do this by selecting the highest quality and highest potential applicants for our future programs.

Our program doesn't only teach you how to write a book – our team of coaches, developmental editors, copy editors, art directors, and marketing experts incubate you from having a book idea to being a published, bestselling author, ensuring that the book you create can actually make a difference in the world. Then we give you the training you need to use your book to make the difference in the world, or to create a business out of serving your readers.

ARE YOU READY TO MAKE A DIFFERENCE?

You've seen other people make a difference with a book. Now it's your turn. If you are ready to stop watching and start taking massive action, go to http://theauthorincubator.com/apply/.

"Yes, I'm ready!"

Other Books by Difference Press

Am I the Reason I'm Not Getting Pregnant?: The Fearlessly Fertile Method for Clearing the Blocks between You and Your Baby
by Rosanne Austin, JD, PCC

Career or Fibromyalgia, Do I Have To Choose?: The Practical Approach to Managing Symptoms and the Life You Love
by Karen R. Brinklow

Damsel No More!: The Secret to Slaying Your Anxiety and Loving Again after an Abusive Relationship
by Emily Davis

Help! My Husband Is Hardly Home: 8 Steps to Feel Supported While Raising Your Family
by Kelsey Domiana

The Divorced Mom Makeover: Rise Up, Reclaim Your Life, and Rock On with Your Gorgeous Self
by Jamie Hernandez

The Right Franchise for You: Escape the 9 to 5, Generate Wealth,
& Live Life on Your Terms
by Faizun Kamal

Overcome Thyroid Symptoms & Love Your Life: The Personal
Guide to Renewal & Re-Calibration
by Vannette Keast

The Luminary Journey: Lessons from a Volcano in Creating
a Healing Center and Becoming the Leader You
Were Born to Be
by Darshan Mendoza

The End Is Near: Planning the Life You Want after the
Kids Are Gone
by Amie Eyre Newhouse

When Marriage Needs an Answer: The Decision to Fix Your
Struggling Marriage or Leave Without Regret
by Sharon Pope

Leadership through Trust & Collaboration: Practical
Tools for Today's Results-Driven Leader
by Jill Ratliff

Conquer Foot Pain: The Art of Eliminating Pain by
Improving Posture so You Can Exercise Again
by Julie Renae Smith, MPT

The Art of Connected Leadership: The Manager's Guide for Keeping Rock Stars and Building Powerhouse Teams
by Lyndsay K. R. Toensing

Financial Freedom for Six-Figure Entrepreneurs: Lower Taxes, Build Wealth, Create Your Best Life
by Jennifer Vavricka

BAD (Begin Again Differently): 7 Smart Processes to Win Again after Suffereing a Business Loss
by Claudette Yarbrough

The Joy of Letting Go of Your Biomedical Career: The Ultimate Quitter's Guide to Flourish without the Burnout
by Xuemei Zhong